Angels and Beasts

Angels and Beasts

The Relationship between the Four Living Creatures
and the Four Riders in Revelation 6:1–8

LAURENȚIU FLORENTIN MOȚ

WIPF & STOCK · Eugene, Oregon

ANGELS AND BEASTS
The Relationship between the Four Living Creatures and the Four Riders in Revelation 6:1–8

Copyright © 2017 Laurențiu Florentin Moț. All rights reserved. Except for brief quotations in critical publications or reviews, no part of this book may be reproduced in any manner without prior written permission from the publisher. Write: Permissions, Wipf and Stock Publishers, 199 W. 8th Ave., Suite 3, Eugene, OR 97401.

Wipf & Stock
An Imprint of Wipf and Stock Publishers
199 W. 8th Ave., Suite 3
Eugene, OR 97401

www.wipfandstock.com

PAPERBACK ISBN: 978-1-5326-1235-0
HARDCOVER ISBN: 978-1-5326-1237-4
EBOOK ISBN: 978-1-5326-1236-7

Manufactured in the U.S.A.   03/01/17

With huge thanks to my wife, Adelina, my son, Darius,
and to the One staying in the shadow of John's vision
and breaking the seven seals.

Contents

Introduction | ix

CHAPTER 1
Textual, Structural, and Contextual Issues | 1
    Translation with Textual and Syntactical Remarks | 1
    The Unit of the First Four Seals | 4
    The Sealed Book | 8
    Rev 3:21 and the Removal of the Seals | 13

CHAPTER 2
The First Century Relevancy of Revelation 6:1–8 | 14
    The Greco-Roman Understanding of Cherubim | 16
    The Judeo-Christian Background of Cherubim and Horsemen | 18
        Old Testament Background for the Four Living Creatures | 19
        Old Testament Background for the Four Riders | 29
    The Old Testament Background of the Seven Seals | 39
        Curses against God's People | 39
        Curses against God's Enemies | 41
    The New Testament Background of Revelation 6:1–8 | 43

CHAPTER 3
The Four Living Creatures as Individuals | 45
    The Order of the Four Living Creatures in Revelation 6:1–8 | 48
    The Meaning of the Order of the Cherubim | 51

    The Living Creatures Understood Individually | 55
    The Lion | 56
    The Ox | 57
    The Man | 59
    The Eagle | 62

CHAPTER 4
Controlling The Four Riders | 65
    The Lion-Cherub Leads the First Rider | 66
    The Ox-Cherub Leads the Second Rider | 70
    The Man-Cherub Leads the Third Rider | 74
    The Vulture-Cherub Leads the Fourth Rider | 77

Conclusion | 81
Bibliography | 85

Introduction

As apocalyptic literature, the book of Revelation was often an attraction for scholars and lay people alike. Its students can hardly say they have reached the end of its meaning. Reading, examining, and practicing the instructions in the book of Revelation will result in great blessing, according to its author (Rev 1:3). It is also true that erroneous conclusions lead to bad decisions in real life, as happened to the group of 130 persons at Waco, Texas, in 1993. They called themselves "Students of the Seven Seals." The sect of the Branch Davidians was led by Vernon Howell's fallacious interpretation of Revelation.[1] His code name, David Koresh, speaks of the sect's messianic-apocalyptic nature. In that case, the study of the seven seals proved to be infelicitous, ending up in a siege having 76 people dying in a series of gun fire and conflagration. Notwithstanding, the passage regarding the seven seals is not as dangerous as that makes it seem. On a sound exegetical basis and with a proper approach, the passage of the seals repays the reader in terms of theology and practical spirituality.

This study deals with the seven seals, particularly the first four. The analysis focuses on the relationship between the four living creatures and the four riders in Rev 6:1–8. For some scholars this relationship is either not existent or hardly visible.[2] Yet, as R.

---

1. Michaels, *Revelation*.

2. E.g., Thomas states: "no correspondence of each seal's content with the likeness of each living being is detectable." *Revelation 1–7*, 415.

INTRODUCTION

H. Charles long ago saw,[3] a quick reading of the text reveals that each of the four riders is called into action by one of the four living creatures that stand in the proximity of God's throne. The identity of the four living creatures in Rev 6:1–8 will be compared to the more detailed description in Rev 4:6–8. Are the living ones introduced in the same order? Is the first living creature in Rev 6:1 the same first living one that looks like a lion in Rev 4:7? What about the other three? Then the research moves toward some other questions: Is there any theological relationship between the lion-featured cherub and the rider it calls in? Likewise, has the ox-featured cherub anything in common with the activity of the rider it controls? These kinds of inquiries will be addressed in relation to the other two cherub-rider teams, also.

Issues such as living creatures and the categories with which they conjoin, horses, riders, and their activities will expand the exploration. Those elements that are relevant to our investigation will be studied, commencing with their Old and New Testament backgrounds and moving toward their context in Revelation. It must be remembered that "the most obvious source of ideas and mental images [for the study of Revelation] is the Old Testament."[4] Books such as Daniel, Ezekiel, Zechariah, Isaiah, Jeremiah, and many other major events from biblical history are, along with some New Testament references on eschatology, the milieu of the meanings that stand behind the scenes of Revelation.

J. Du Rand is correct when he argues that the unique relevance of Revelation within the NT frame lies in the fact that "it offers the contemporary Christian reader historical and eschatological insights about the past, present and future," alongside a theological perspective about God's judgmental and salvific actions in the

---

3. "The first four [seals] possess one characteristic in common—the impersonation of their leading features: another is their connection with the four living beings." Charles, *A Critical and Exegetical Commentary on the Revelation of St John*, 171.

4. D. Guthrie, *New Testament Introduction*, 965. Guthrie says the following: "Indeed so basic is the Old Testament to the writer's mental concepts that out of 404 verses in the entire book there are only 126 which contain no allusion to it" (966).

world.[5] That is why understanding the relationship between the four living creatures and the four riders in Rev 6:1–8 would expand not only our understanding of the seven seals but also make Revelation speak to the current world, by bringing in the present, both the past and future.

5. du Rand, *Johannine Perspectives*, 192.

CHAPTER 1

Textual, Structural, and Contextual Issues

TRANSLATION WITH TEXTUAL AND SYNTACTICAL REMARKS

THE PASSAGE READS AS follows: "1 And I looked as the lamb opened the first[1] of the seven seals and I heard the first of the four living

1. "The first of the seven seals" is the correct rendition, albeit we must mention that literally it stands for "*one* of the seven seals." There are some definite examples which prove that whenever the cardinal adjective "εἷς, μία, ἕν" precedes ordinal adjectives (δεύτερος, τρίτος, τέταρτος, etc.) it also gets an ordinal sense, to be translated "the first"; Titus 3:10; Rev 6:1 (cf. v. 3); 9:12 (cf. 11:14). This is why in the same verse, the phrase "*one* of the seven seals" (μίαν ἐκ τῶν ἑπτὰ σφραγίδων) must by necessity be translated "the first of the seven seals." In both cases, the rationale of interpreting "one of" by "the first of" is grounded in the context. The next living creatures, as well as the next seals, are identified as "the second, the third, etc."

creatures as[2] a voice like thunder, saying: 'Come!'[3] 2 And I looked and behold, a white horse, and the one sitting on it having a bow, and it was given to him a crown[4] and went out conquering and in order to conquer. 3 When He opened the second seal, I heard the second living creature saying: 'Come!' 4 And another horse, red,[5] came out and it was given[6] to the one sitting on it to take peace

---

2. Some versions hide the comparing force of the conjunction ὡς, in expressions such as "in a thundering voice" (CJB), "in a voice like thunder" (NAB, NIV), "with a thunderous voice" (NET), "with a voice like thunder" (NLT). The idea is that the voice that John heard seemed to him somewhat like a thunder in volume and intensity. The thunder is a comparison here, not an adjective which qualifies the noun "voice."

3. The calling is not addressed to John, as TR (καὶ βλέπε), followed by GNV, KJV, WEB, YLT, TNT, L45, MGK, puts it, but to the first rider who comes up in the scenario. It is the same case with regards to the other three riders (Rev 6:3, 5, 7). The appeal could also be translated imperatively as "Go!" See Bruce M. Metzger, *A Textual Commentary on the Greek New Testament* (Stuttgart: German Bible Society, 1994), 667. The following witnesses add to "ἔρχου" a variation of the same urge "καὶ ἴδε" ("and see"): Codex Sinaiticus Petropolitanus; Cod. Vaticanus nr. 2066; Manuscripts of *Koine* tradition; the first Monophysite Syriac version (Philoxeniana), partially survived; and Vulgata (Editio Clementina).

4. The crown in view here is a στέφανος, the crown of the victorious athlete, fundamentally different from διάδημα, the royal crown. Semantically, the point made by the author is that the rider is only partially victorious. The victory is progressive. The battle has not come to its end, but only to the first triumph. This is confirmed by the syntax, since the rider came "in order to conquer" more.

5. Πυρρός means the color of fire, red as fire. It was the regular way to express in Hellenistic Greek the red color. That is why the element of fire is semantically forceless. It merely serves as a metaphor, expressing nothing about the nature of the object described as fiery red. John did not see a blazing horse, but simply a red one.

6. ἐδόθη αὐτῷ, lit. "it was given to"; the idiom expresses permission from a higher authority (cf. Rev 8:3; 9:1; 13:5, 7; 13:14–15; 16:8). Most often this authority is God's (e.g., "you would have no power over me if it were not given to you from above," εἰ μὴ ἦν δεδομένον σοι ἄνωθεν, John 19:11). The pronoun is redundant since it refers back to τῷ καθημένῳ ἐπ' αὐτόν. However, this redundancy is acceptable in constructions with *casus pendens* like this one. In other words, the word order requires the repetition of the pronoun, although this pronoun is strictly speaking not syntactically needed.

Textual, Structural, and Contextual Issues

away from the earth in order that they will slay[7] one another and a large sword[8] was given to him. 5 When He opened the third seal, I heard the third living creature saying: 'Come!' 6 And I looked and behold, a black horse and the one sitting on it having a scale[9] in his hand. 7 And I heard like a voice[10] in the middle of the four living creatures saying: 'a quart of wheat for a denarius[11] and three quarts of barley for a denarius, but do not harm[12] either the oil, or the wine.' 8 When He opened the fourth seal, I heard the voice of

---

7. σφάξουσιν, verb indicative future active 3rd person plural from σφάζω, to slaughter, either animals or persons. In LXX it is the technical term for "sacrifice" (Exod 12:6; Lev 1:11; 3:13; 4:15, 24, 29, 33; 6:18; 7:2; 14:5, 13; 17:5; Num 19:3; Ezek 44:11). In the context referring to persons, the implication is of violence and mercilessness—"to slaughter, to kill." But there is a relationship between the act of killing, which is unreligious and its significance, which might be religious. Those slaughtered are in a sense "sacrificed." Since God does not receive human sacrifices (Gen 22:11–12; cf. Lev 18:21; 2 Kgs 23:10; Jer 7:31; 19:5) those slaughtered are offered to another deity. Or the act of taking their life comes from a religious motivation, clearly not from God.

8. μάχαιρα, ης, ἡ, originally a large knife for killing and cutting up; in the NT *sword, saber*; literally, as a curved weapon for close combat *(small) sword, dagger* (John 18:11); figuratively, as a symbol of violent death (Rom 8:35), of hostility (Matt 10:34), of the power of life and death (Rom 13:4).

9. From ζυγός, yoke; balance, scales. In the near context it better fits the latter meaning (see the next verse), although the former hints to the idea of oppressiveness that might cause poverty, which is affirmed afterwards.

10. One may wonder why the verb ἀκούειν takes in Rev 6:7 a direct object in the accusative (φωνὴν τοῦ τετάρτου ζῴου) whereas in vv. 1, 3, and 5 the direct object is every time in the genitive (ἑνὸς ἐκ τῶν τεσσάρων ζῴων, τοῦ δευτέρου ζῴου, τοῦ τρίτου ζῴου). The explanation comes from classical Greek where the verb "to hear" deviated from the rule, which stated that verbs of sensation always take direct objects in the accusative. The rule was that the speaker was rendered in the genitive, while the speech was "heard" in the accusative. In Rev 6:1–8, John is classical in this respect. In vv. 1, 3, and 5 he refers to the sources of speech, so the genitive is regular. In v. 7, however, he points to the voice produced or the content spoken by the fourth living creature. In this case, the accusative is expected.

11. Literally δηναρίου, a denarius, Roman silver coin equivalent to the day's wage of a common laborer, so a day's remuneration for work. See Matt 20:1–12.

12. Ἀδικέω, to hurt or to harm, to treat unjustly, with the implication of doing something which is wrong and undeserved. The word is used with reference to judgments upon the evildoers and persecution of Christians.

Angels and Beasts

the third living creature saying: 'Come!' And I looked and behold a pale[13] horse, and the one siting above it; his name is Death and Hades[14] follows after him. Authority was given to them over the fourth of the earth to kill with sword, famine, plague,[15] and by the beasts of the earth."[16]

THE UNIT OF THE FIRST FOUR SEALS

The literary plan of Revelation is seen differently by scholars. The possible arrangements of Revelation "vary perhaps more than with any other book of the Bible."[17] Among scholars there is agreement on this issue, namely that Revelation can be structured in different

  13. Χλωρός, greenish-yellow (like young grass or leaves), pale-green, light-green, green, grassy, yellowish. The term stands many times for vegetation and so expressing the green color. However, the context in Rev 6:7 does not allow for this sense.
  14. Death and the place of the dead are here personified.
  15. Literally θανάτω, which strictly means 'death', but also has the sense of plague, calamity. The second occurrence of θάνατος is put, by metonymy, as the effect for the cause producing it, which is pestilence. We call the oriental plague that raged in Europe in the 14th century the "black death" by the same figure of speech.
  16. My translation. Unless otherwise stated, all translations are from the NIV. The Greek text in NA28 is: Καὶ εἶδον ὅτε ἤνοιξεν τὸ ἀρνίον μίαν ἐκ τῶν ἑπτὰ σφραγίδων, καὶ ἤκουσα ἑνὸς ἐκ τῶν τεσσάρων ζῴων λέγοντος ὡς φωνὴ βροντῆς· ἔρχου. 2 καὶ εἶδον, καὶ ἰδοὺ ἵππος λευκός, καὶ ὁ καθήμενος ἐπ' αὐτὸν ἔχων τόξον καὶ ἐδόθη αὐτῷ στέφανος καὶ ἐξῆλθεν νικῶν καὶ ἵνα νικήσῃ. 3 Καὶ ὅτε ἤνοιξεν τὴν σφραγῖδα τὴν δευτέραν, ἤκουσα τοῦ δευτέρου ζῴου λέγοντος· ἔρχου. 4 καὶ ἐξῆλθεν ἄλλος ἵππος πυρρός, καὶ τῷ καθημένῳ ἐπ' αὐτὸν ἐδόθη αὐτῷ λαβεῖν τὴν εἰρήνην ἐκ τῆς γῆς καὶ ἵνα ἀλλήλους σφάξουσιν καὶ ἐδόθη αὐτῷ μάχαιρα μεγάλη. 5 Καὶ ὅτε ἤνοιξεν τὴν σφραγῖδα τὴν τρίτην, ἤκουσα τοῦ τρίτου ζῴου λέγοντος· ἔρχου. καὶ εἶδον, καὶ ἰδοὺ ἵππος μέλας, καὶ ὁ καθήμενος ἐπ' αὐτὸν ἔχων ζυγὸν ἐν τῇ χειρὶ αὐτοῦ. 6 καὶ ἤκουσα ὡς φωνὴν ἐν μέσῳ τῶν τεσσάρων ζῴων λέγουσαν· χοῖνιξ σίτου δηναρίου καὶ τρεῖς χοίνικες κριθῶν δηναρίου, καὶ τὸ ἔλαιον καὶ τὸν οἶνον μὴ ἀδικήσῃς. 7 Καὶ ὅτε ἤνοιξεν τὴν σφραγῖδα τὴν τετάρτην, ἤκουσα φωνὴν τοῦ τετάρτου ζῴου λέγοντος· ἔρχου. 8 καὶ εἶδον, καὶ ἰδοὺ ἵππος χλωρός, καὶ ὁ καθήμενος ἐπάνω αὐτοῦ ὄνομα αὐτῷ [ὁ] θάνατος, καὶ ὁ ᾅδης ἠκολούθει μετ' αὐτοῦ καὶ ἐδόθη αὐτοῖς ἐξουσία ἐπὶ τὸ τέταρτον τῆς γῆς ἀποκτεῖναι ἐν ῥομφαίᾳ καὶ ἐν λιμῷ καὶ ἐν θανάτῳ καὶ ὑπὸ τῶν θηρίων τῆς γῆς. (Rev 6:1–8).
  17. Osborne, *Revelation*, 29.

ways. This is not due to the preferences of various scholars. The reason for the many structural schemes seems to be that "the sections relate at more than one level."[18] Researchers argue for many types of arrangements. Most of these are included in the following list: David Aune promotes a bipartite structure of Revelation, based on Rev 1:19 (1:9–3:22, the theophany of the exalted Christ; 4:1–22:9, a series of visions introduced by pictures from heaven);[19] Ranko Stefanović creates a threefold structure of Revelation (messages to the seven churches, [Rev 1:9–3:22], where Christ is presented as a high priest; opening of the sealed scroll [Rev 4–11], where Christ appears as the eschatological ruler; and contents of the sealed scroll [Rev 12–22:5], a section that displays Christ as the apocalyptic Michael);[20] four groups of seven "determine the whole structure and message of the book," states Eugenio Corsini;[21] Jacques Ellul sees a five-fold structure around the five sevens observed in the book (the churches, the seals, the trumpets, the bowls, the group of visions introduced with the "I saw" formula);[22] Merrill Tenney suggests six sections for dividing Revelation (1:1–8, Prologue—Christ talks; 1:9–3:22, Christ in the church; 4:1–16:21, Christ in heaven; 17:1–21:2, Christ conquers; 21:9–22:5, Christ crowned; 22:6–21, Epilogue—Christ calls).[23] Revelation was also divided into seven and eight parts by Gregory Beale[24] and Adela Yabro Collins.[25]

At the same time, it seems fairly clear that Revelation contains some well-defined structural divisions. The seven seals is one of these. As the text flows it becomes also evident that the first four seals are set apart from the final three. In favor of this are the very scenes in the vision of the seven seals. The scenes in the first four seals deal with four horsemen, while the last three are different.

18. Ibid.
19. Aune, *Revelation 1–5*, 100–105.
20. Stefanović, *Revelation*, 42.
21. Corsini, *Apocalypse*, 62–63.
22. Ellul, *Apocalypse*, 36–45.
23. Tenney, *Privire de ansamblu*, 355–57.
24. Beale, *Book of Revelation*, 114–15.
25. Collins, *Combat Myth*, 13–39.

The entire process of breaking the seals causes various types of judgments. The first four represent a general picture of the process of divine discipline. They do not target a specific sin. The fifth and sixth seals illustrate God's response to a more specific category, namely, those who are hostile to Him and His people.

The separation of the first four seals from the last three is not unnatural. Moreover, the distinction bears a certain significance, when one reads the first four seals with the basic meaning of the number four in mind. Among Bible numerals, number four indicates completeness,[26] "an incomparable symbol of plenitude and universality."[27] Strictly applied to Rev 6:1–8, the number four

---

26. Walker, "Four," *International Standard Bible Encyclopedia*, 2:357. See for instance the four rivers of Paradise in Gen 2:10; "the four winds of heaven" in Ezek 37:9; Dan 7:2; 8:8; 11:4; Zech 6:5; "the four winds" in Matt 24:31; Mark 13:27; "the four corners of the earth" in Isa 11:12; Rev 7:1; 20:8; and "the four corners of the house" in Job 1:19.

27. Gheerbrant, *Dicționar de simboluri*, 29. "Four" was a sacred and complete number with the Jews, as well as with several other peoples. It occurs very frequently in the Old and New Testaments. We have the four rivers of Paradise (Gen 2:10); the four winds of heaven (Ezek 37:9; Dan 7:2; 8:8; 11:4; Zech 6:5); "the four winds" (Matt 24:31; Mark 13:27); "the four corners of the earth" (Isa 11:12; Rev 7:1; 20:8); "the four corners of the house" (Job 1:19); Jephthah's daughter was bewailed four days a year (Judg 11:40); "four cities" are several times mentioned in Joshua in the allotment of inheritances (19:7; 21:18, etc.); Nehemiah's enemies sent to him "four times" (Neh 6:4); "four kinds" of destroyers were threatening (Jer 15:3); Yahweh has "four sore judgments" (Ezek 14:21); "four generations" were seen by Job after his recovery (42:16). "Four" is frequent in the prophetic portions of biblical literature: Daniel saw "four . . . beasts" arise, representing four kings (7:3, 17); "four notable horns" (8:8, 22; compare 2 Esdr 11:39); "four horns" were seen by Zechariah, as the powers that had scattered Israel; "four chariots and . . . horses" represented the "four spirits," that went "forth from standing before the Lord of all the earth" (Zech 6:1–5); in the visions of Ezekiel, "four living creatures," each with four faces, four wings, etc., were the bearers of the throne of God (1:5 f., 23); so, in the visions of John there were "four living creatures" before and around the throne (Rev 4:6; 5:6, 8, 14; 6:1; 15:7; 19:4); John saw "four angels" of destruction loosed for their work (Rev 9:14 f.). "Four" occurs frequently in the measurements of the sacred buildings, etc. (1) of the tabernacle (Exod 25; 26; 27; 28:17; 36, etc.); (2) of Solomon's temple (1 Kgs 7:2, etc.; 1 Chr 9:24); (3) of Ezekiel's temple (Ezek 40:41; 41:5; 42:20; 43:14, etc.). "Four" is used as an alternative with "three" (Prov 30:15, 18, 21, 24, 29); we have "three or four" (2 Esdr 16:29, 31); "the third and . . . the fourth generation" (Exod 20:5; 34:7;

would suggest that the living creature-rider teams involved in the vision have together a complete mission. Within the section of the seven seals, the first four seals appears to be a freestanding coherent group. "This is obvious in view of the stereotypical structure with variations that characterize the brief narrative describing the breaking of the first four seals."[28] We find four living creatures, four riders, and four penalties. Their manifestations, actions, and roles have universal consequences. Completeness is achieved through the activity of each of the four teams, which cumulatively add to the picture.

When the second horse enters the stage, the first one seems to be still running. This appears to stand so on account of the following arguments: (1) first of all, the number "four" means completeness, while fewer than "four" means incompleteness; (2) second, as Jon Paulien remarks, "each [rider] affects only a quarter of the earth (6:8). Thus the 'judgments' of the horsemen are partial and restrained."[29] But together they make the whole; (3) third, the description of the first rider as "conquering and in order to conquer" (Rev 6:2) means that his crown of victory expresses only a partial success, to be made complete in the process.

This feature of the seven seals looks to be shared with the section of the seven trumpets. Both sevens are divided into four elements followed by three. Rev 8:13 states: "And I looked, and I heard an eagle flying in midair saying with a loud voice: 'Woe! Woe! Woe to the inhabitants of the earth, because of the remaining trumpet blasts of the three angels who are about to sound!'" The last three trumpets call for special attention. They are different from the first four. In both seals and trumpets, the fifth episode introduces a special category: the martyrs (in the case of the seven seals) and "those people who do not have the seal of God on their foreheads" (in the case of the seven trumpets; see Rev 9:4). The passage of the first four seals depicts the work of the heavenly

---

Num 14:18; Deut 5:9).

28. Aune, *Revelation 6–16*, 389.

29. Paulien, "Seven Seals," 234.

beings and the relationship between them in the course of their universal mission.

THE SEALED BOOK

The first four seals passage (Rev 6:1–8) indicates that everything is thrown in motion by the condition of the scroll in Rev 5. The document needs to be opened and this necessitates the intervention of the Lamb, the only one who has the authority to break its seals (cf. Rev 5:2–5). The removal of the first four seals generates a certain cause and effect chain. A certain living creature commands a correspondent rider to take action. The horsemen accomplish their job, and the removing of the seals will totally assuage John's grief (cf. Rev 5:5). Meanwhile, the same action brings punishment upon earth with an increasing intensity.

That the Lamb removes the seals signifies that the scroll belongs to Him. Stefanović states, "It seems that the fundamental message of something sealed was that it was 'owned' by whoever sealed it."[30] Also, he adds that "only the owner could break the seals [of a document] and disclose the content."[31] The release of seals of the scroll is parallel with the release of the horsemen. As Christ owns the document and has power over it, so the four living creatures exercise authority over the four riders and are in charge of them. The background of Rev 6:1–8, so vital to its proper interpretation, is the background of the seven seals. This milieu is to be established in accordance with the general structure of the book. The literary analysis of the Johannine Apocalypse done by Kenneth Strand has demonstrated that the literary arrangement of Revelation is basically chiastic.[32] He divides the book into eight basic sections or visions, beginning with a prologue, and ending with an epilogue. Building on Strand's investigation, both Richard

---

30. Stefanović, *Sealed Book of Revelation 5*, 130. In the context, God seems to be the One who sealed the book, while Christ is He who opens it.

31. Ibid., 134; cf. Isa 29:11.

32. Strand, "The Eight Basic Visions," and "'Victorious Introduction' Scenes," 35–72.

M. Davidson and Jon Paulien argue for a sevenfold structure of Revelation. Their conclusion is that the book contains seven basic visions, each one being preceded by an introductory sanctuary scene.[33] Consequently, the scene with the opening of the seven seals (Rev 6:1–8:1) is defined by the sanctuary setting of Rev 4–5.

In Rev 4 the reader meets an atmosphere of exultation and rejoice declared in worship songs and praise. Engaged in adoration and homage are the four living creatures, twenty-four elders, many angels, and, finally, the entire creation. The four living creatures are the leaders of worship services (cf. 4:8). Everything they do is a constant exaltation of God's holiness.

A contrasting issue breaks the gala beginning with Rev 5:1. This chapter contains the vision of the sealed book,[34] and the perspective of Christ opening it, which occasions universal joy among all ranks and sorts of creatures. First, a declaration is issued, that none could be found in heaven, on earth, or under the earth to perform such a task. This statement impressed John so much that it made him weep. He was comforted only when one of the elders assured him that there was a person who could open the book, and would do it, whose title is the Lion of the tribe of Judah, and the root of David, which are Messianic names.[35] After John stops

---

33. Davidson, "Sanctuary Typology," 112–15; Paulien, "Seals and Trumpets," 187–88.

34. The practice of sealing was common in the biblical world and in the Roman Empire. Romans had a law through which a document had to be sealed by seven witnesses (five common witnesses and two praetorians). The praetorians should have confirmed whether the alleged heir is the son of the testator or not. Also, they had to authenticate whether the proponent was worthy of inheritance, being in proper relationships with the laws of the 12 bronze plates promulgated in the Forum (for more information see Maine, *Ancient Law*, 1861, http://socserv.mcmaster.ca/~econ/ugcm/3ll3/maine/anclaw/chap06). Revelation 6:14 reveals what John understood by "βιβλίον," "book"—"The sky receded like a scroll, rolling up, and every mountain and island was removed from its place." The term "scroll" is a parchment, not a codex (the ancient name of the modern book) whose mention starts in the second century A.D., while John receives the Revelation in the late first century A.D.

35. See Gen 49:9, 10; Isa 11:1, 10; Heb 7:14.

weeping, the joyful songs are resumed and praise reaches cosmic dimensions (Rev 5:9, 10, 12–13).

The basic idea of Rev 4–5 is praise and adoration of God and the Lamb. Both of them are worthy; the former because He is the Creator and the latter because of His recent, redeeming death. A sealed book in this context is a human crisis. Only John is weeping. The work of the four Living Creatures and of the four riders that follow the breaking of the seals is to be interpreted from this perspective. The work of the four teams expresses the two qualities of God, that of Creator and Redeemer. In their mission, the four teams manipulate creation, or nature, trying to return people to God in order to be ransomed.

With this biblical background in mind, John understands that the sealed book is a record of humanity.[36] In the context of Revelation, the book, a generic document, has to be related to the book of life owned by Christ (cf. Rev 13:5);[37] the fact that nobody

---

36. The ancients had the custom of keeping genealogical records (Neh 7:5, 64; 12:22, 23) and of enrolling citizens for various purposes (Jer 22:30; Ezek 13:9). So, God is represented as having a record of all who are under His special care and guardianship. Moses is written in God's book, which corresponds with the assurance of eternal life but is not an unmovable destiny (Exod 32:32; Ps 69:28). In the New Testament it is the record of the righteous who are to inherit eternal life (Phil 4:3; Rev 3:5; 13:8; 17:8; 21:27). In the apocalyptic writings there is the conception of a book or of books, that are in God's keeping, and upon which the final judgment is to be based (Dan 7:10; 12:1; Rev 20:12, 15); Cf. Book of Jubilees 39:6; 19:9. In 39:6, for instance, somebody can read about Joseph when he refused the indecent proposal of Potiphar's wife the following: "But he [Joseph] did not surrender his soul, and he remembered the Lord and the words which Jacob, his father, used to read from amongst the words of Abraham, that no man should commit fornication with a woman who hath a husband; that for him the punishment of death hath been ordained in the heavens before the Most High God, and the sin will be recorded against him in the *eternal books* continually before the Lord." Charles, *Apocrypha and Pseudepigrapha*, 185. Italics mine.

37. Revelation 3:5 evokes the book of life theme for the first time in Revelation. The second time John uses the symbol is in 13:8 where he adds a crucial detail. The parchment is depicted as pertaining to the Lamb. The apostle uses the expression "the book of life *belonging to* the Lamb." What happened between Rev 3:5 and 13:8 that made him say this? The answer is found in Rev 5. The gesture of picking up the sealed book from God's right hand is the clue.

has access to the book means that those recorded in the book are in danger unless Christ intervenes. There is no one to assume the record which contains data about human beings in regard to God's laws and conduct. Jesus Christ, the recently slain Lamb, is the only one who can take responsibility for those listed in the book. That is the reason why He is praised as Redeemer[38] and King. He redeemed them of their debts while the debtors became His property. He is the one who rules.

The scene of Rev 5 speaks about the Lamb who is enthroned after his sacrifice.[39] The ceremony of enthronement in the Old Testament contained an episode when the king was supposed to receive a book of covenant (cf. 2 Kgs 11:12–19; 2 Chr 23:11–20). That is why the book[40] the Lamb holds functions like the book

---

Christ takes responsibility for what is written in the book. The association of Jesus' sacrifice with the concept of redemption in Rev 5 (see v. 9) demonstrates that the Lamb's blood removes the debts of those written in the book. They were ransomed, so after the Rev 5 ceremony, the book pertains to the Lamb.

38. Christ is the *Go'el*, the closest kindred which, according to the Law (Lev 25:47–49; Job 19:23–27; Ruth 4) had two functions: he had the right to redeem (to become the owner) and to avenge his killed family members (Josh 20:1–9; compare with the fifth seal [Rev 6:9–11] where the martyrs cry out to be avenged).

39. Ranko Stefanović indicates that "the description of the scene in Revelation 5 is patterned after the Old Testament coronation and enthronement ceremony (cf. 2 Kgs 11:12–19; 2 Chr 23:11–20)." Stefanović, *Revelation*, 161. In the Old Testament prophetic books, phrases and terms like "throne," "at the right hand," "the Lion from the tribe of Judah," "the Root of David," and "worthy," all of them present in Rev 5, are used frequently with reference to the future, ideal king of David's lineage who will sit on David's seat. Stefanović sees the usage of these terms in Rev 5 as a "fulfillment of the Old Testament promise with regard to the exaltation of Jesus Christ, the promised Davidic descendent, on the throne of the Universe" (ibid., 198). Understood in this way, Rev 5 depicts the sealed scroll as a symbol of rulership. It appears to be the document of God's eternal covenant between Him and all believing in Christ as Redeemer. Those included in the covenant are not predestined to salvation and steadfastness, but they could nullify the covenant by unfaithfulness. What is sure is that the parchment contains their names, so they are the property of the Lamb.

40. The document has no title that is why it is a generic and symbolic one. Ellen White agrees when she says: "There in His open hand lay the book, the roll of the history of God's providences, the prophetic history of nations and

of the covenant. The covenant contains blessings and curses associated with people's faithfulness or disloyalty. For instance, after Solomon's coronation, David commissioned his son to kill two perfidious and subversive servants, but, at the same time, to show kindness to other good servants (1 Kgs 2:5–9). Both categories are on the emperor's agenda. Ranko Stefanović vividly observes:

> When in the Old Testament the newly crowned king took his place on the throne, the destiny of the entire nation was placed in his hands. The Old Testament enthronement ceremonies were usually followed by judgment actions of a newly enthroned king when he proceeded to punish those who had proven disloyal and rebellious; he would also bestow favorable benefits on the loyal adherents (cf. 1 Kgs 2; 16:11; 2 Kgs 9:14–10:27; 11:1, 13–16). In royal Psalms 2 and 110, which originally referred to the Israelite kings, the anointed and enthroned Davidic king was to exercise authority to reign by judgment those who were rebellious (compare Ps 2:7–11 and Rev 19:15–16). This judgment aspect is expressed in the vision of the opening of the seven seals.[41]

Revelation 6:1–8 comes after Christ's investiture as King. The breaking of the seals causes the four living creatures to summon the riders of judgment upon His servants. These are preliminary judgments (Rev 6:8). Along the paradigm of Solomon who did not kill Joab and Shimei immediately, but tested them (1 Kgs 2:13–46), the seven seals unfold a progression in the intensity of discipline. The four living creatures along with the four riders are agents of a progressive penalty.

---

the church. Herein was contained the divine utterances, His authority, His commandments, His laws, the whole symbolic counsel of the Eternal, and the history of all ruling powers in the nations. In symbolic language was contained in that roll the influence of every nation, tongue, and people from the beginning of earth's history to its close." White, *Manuscript Releases*, 9:667.

41. Stefanović, *Revelation*, 214–15.

REV 3:21 AND THE REMOVAL OF THE SEALS

The key text to understanding the seals is Rev 3:21. It is a promise to the conqueror in Laodicea to sit with Jesus on His throne, as Christ overcame and sat with His Father on His throne. Chapter 4 prepares for the enthronement of Jesus in chapter 5, which Rev 3:21 talks about. The promise remains unfulfilled as long as there are no conquerors. The seventh chapter delineates a special group of victors (the 144,000) in the final spiritual battle who will later be enthroned (Rev 20:4). Thus, "the six seals lie between the victory of the Lamb predicted in chapter 5 and of the saints in chapter 7."[42]

In this pattern chapter 6 corresponds to the process of overcoming. Thus, the seals plainly create the battlefield of discipline through which the church will become spotless and pure. In this spiritual arena many true followers of Jesus are slain because of their faith. The question, "How long" will pass until they will be justified, is soon to be answered. As George Ladd says:

> Before the final judgment falls, God will pour out a series of woes upon those who are seduced by these evil powers. These judgments will not only manifest the wrath of God against all evil and rebellion but will also have the merciful purpose of driving the wicked to their knees in repentance before final judgment falls and it is too late.[43]

The question "Who is able to stand?" (Rev 6:17) is overdue. The wicked are concerned with the matter of standing too late. If repentance comes at the dawn of the second coming of Jesus, it comes in vain. Seemingly, with each seal removed, time passes. The direction is Christ's second coming. The most important issue at that time is the question of spiritual standing. By their authority over the four riders, the four living creatures command actions that promote the spiritual growth of people, to prepare and train them for the Lord's Day.

---

42. Ford, *Revelation*, 101.
43. Ladd, *Revelation of John*, 95.

CHAPTER 2

The First Century Relevancy of Revelation 6:1–8

SOME MODERN SCHOLARS ENDORSE a literal understanding of the seven seals vision, which leads them to interpret Rev 6:1–8 as a reflection of the first-century situation in the Roman Empire, characterized by warfare.[1] Following this school of thought, the first seal would stand for the Parthians, an enduring menace for Romans during the end of the first century A.D. They were always ready to cross the Euphrates and fight with the Romans. Their boldness resulted in some important victories. The understanding of the other seals goes in the same theological direction, thus suggesting that they represent the political, civil, and physical disorders that undermined the oppressive power of the Roman Empire.[2]

Considering the fact that the Bible is addressed primarily to the people of its time, we may assume that the first-century Christians found contemporary relevance in the sixth chapter of Revelation. But the theology which applies the symbols of Rev 6:1–8 to the wars in the Roman Empire of the first century is defective.[3]

---

1. So Moffat, *Revelation of St. John*, 388–89.
2. Fiorenza, *Apocalypse*, 62–65.
3. Before anything else, the situation in the late first century in the Roman Empire "was not a time particularly characterized by warfare." Ladd,

The First Century Relevancy of Revelation 6:1–8

We assume that before any application in contemporary history, John's hearers searched for meaning in the sacred Hebrew and Christian texts they were familiar with. That is why it is likely that their primary search was for theological meaning. What symbolizes the four living creatures in the apocalyptic literature? Is there any biblical passage which provides background for them? What is their role and status? Are the four riders a familiar symbol for first-century Christians? Can we find a background passage in the older scriptures? At the same time, awareness of the fact that some of the symbols of Rev 6:1–8 (e.g., the four living creatures) were present in the ancient culture is necessary. However, their significance is to be extracted from biblical sources. This assumption is in accordance with the hermeneutical principle that the literary context prevails over the historical context. Not that the latter is less important, but "the literary context presents the most reliable guide for determining the most likely meaning in that setting."[4] We study the text first, that is why the text comes before the historical environment in our interpretation. Our literary framework begins

---

Revelation of John, 100. "The world had not been at peace since the days of Alexander the Great. The quarrels of the Diadochi, and the aggression of the Roman republic had kept the nations in a state of constant turmoil. A universal peace was first established, however, with the beginning of the reign of Augustus and the closing of the temple of Janus. In all the countries round the Mediterranean and from distant Britain to the Euphrates, the world was at rest. This was the great *Pax Romana*. Rome had made an end of her own civil wars and had put a stop to wars among the nations. Though her wars were often iniquitous and unjustifiable, and she conquered like a barbarian, she ruled her conquests like a humane statesman. The quarrels of the Diadochi which caused so much turmoil in the East were ended, the territory of the Lagids, Attalids, Seleucids, and Antigonids having passed under the sway of Rome. The empire united Greeks, Romans, and Jews all under one government." Angus, "Roman Empire and Christianity," 4:210. Also important is that a literal understanding of the seven seals goes against the symbolic character of the Apocalypse. The interpreter must first get the theological meaning of the text, then he should try to find a historical thread, if any. Finally, such an understanding would prove a great discrepancy with the theological framework of the entire book. As Stefanović says, "The theological meaning of Revelation 6 is much deeper than the warfare between the Parthians and the Roman Empire." Stefanović, *Revelation*, 214.

4. Klein, et al., *Biblical Interpretation*, 215.

with the text (Rev 6:1–8) and continues with the immediate context, major section, book, writer, testament, and finally, the whole Bible.[5] Only then should we move towards the historical-cultural background. Also important to mention is that the historical-cultural milieu comes from two main sources: the scriptures and extra-biblical material. The former is paramount, while the latter is secondary.

THE GRECO-ROMAN UNDERSTANDING OF CHERUBIM[6]

People from among non-Jewish nations, even those converted to Christianity, presumably had different backgrounds that gave meaning to cherubim and their role in relation to humanity. Thus, Rev 6:1–8 probably signified different things for the Gentile public or Christians recently converted from among non-Jews. Freedman says, "The many variations of cherubim represented in the Bible— examples with one or more faces; with human, leonine, bovine, or aquiline faces; with two or four legs—correspond to various forms of composite beasts depicted in ANE art, particularly the art of Assyria."[7]

The cherub was considered analogous to the griffin, a name found almost in the same form in Persian and Greek. In ancient Near Eastern mythology, griffins were intermediaries between men and gods, carrying men's prayers up to the higher beings. Cherubim are not described in detail in the Bible and it is known only that they had faces and wings. It is also possible that John's contemporaries of pagan culture and pedigree traced the origin of imagery from the beings depicted in Egyptian paintings as having bodies of young winged boys and girls, or from the Mesopotamian winged bulls, guardians of the temples. They were also represented as sphinxes (lions with human faces and outspread wings touching

---

5. For a detailed discussion see Osborne, *Hermeneutical Spiral*, 21–40.

6. In pagan context, "cherubim" is the term that corresponds to "living creature."

7. Meyers, "Cherubim," 117.

at the back).⁸ "There are numerous representations of sphinxes in the art of Palestine during the Bronze and Iron Ages."⁹ Throughout ancient Egypt, the four genii are described on artifacts and other paleographic remainings as four sphinxes. There is plenty of documentation about this in excerpts from the Great Pyramid or other temples in Egypt (found both in Egyptian and English). The image is that of a lion-headed, bull-headed, eagle-headed sphinx and one with a human head.

An overview of these pagan sources is necessary. A non-Jewish mind could have extracted the meaning of cherubim from the figures of winged creatures, well known in ANE art and religious symbolism. The *Encyclopedia Judaica* testifies:

> Two winged beings flank the throne of Hiram, king of Byblos, and winged bulls were placed at the entrance of Babylonian and Assyrian palaces and templates. They appear on the pottery incense altars from Taanach and Meggido. Winged sphinxes, griffins, and human creatures are represented in the art and iconography of Carchemish, Calah, Minrud, the Samaritan ivories, Aleppo, and Tell Halaf.¹⁰

The Assyrian, Persian, Greek, Egyptian, and Mesopotamian milieus stand as the spring of interpretation to such persons. We see that the cherubim basically fulfill two roles: (1) that of intermediaries between humans and the deity; and (2) that of guardians of the Temple and king. These non-Jewish clues for decoding the

---

8. The griffin (lion-bodied, eagle-faced) and the sphinx (lion-bodied, human-faced, mostly female) were borrowed from the Near East by western religion and art. At first the griffin was thought to be hostile to human beings but gradually this idea changed. It was then consecrated to Apollo and guarded the wine of Dionysus. Both the griffin and the sphinx are frequently represented in Greek, Roman and Hellenistic art, and to a much lesser extent also in Byzantine religious art. This hybrid animal, however, was inherited from the tabernacle and appears hundreds of times in the iconography of western Asia between 1800 and 600 BC. Many representations are found with a deity or king seated on a throne supported by two cherubim (ibid., 117–18).

9. Negev, *Encyclopedia of the Holy Land*.

10. *Encyclopaedia Judaica*, s.v. "Cherub."

imagery of cherubim are general and some of them parallel the angelic features revealed in Revelation. For instance, the mediatory role of the cherubim is found in the Apocalypse,[11] where the four living creatures stand between Christ who breaks the seals and the riders that are activated afterwards to affect humanity by their actions.

Notwithstanding, the ancient Near Eastern mythology which asserts that the cherubim are carrying men's prayers up to God is not specifically found in the Bible. Angels do answer prayers (cf. Dan 9:22–23; Acts 12:11–12), and are somehow engaged in mediation (Job 33:23).[12] But we cannot ascertain the exact nature of their intercession. What is sure, however, is that only Christ is the Mediator for sin between God and humanity (1 Tim 2:5). The picture of angels guarding the Temple or God's throne should not mean that God needs bodyguards or a shield of defense. These mighty beings are described in the familiar language of the ancient world. However, the real significance for them in the book of Revelation has to be drawn from a Judeo-Christian background. The canonical text is to be deciphered by the canonical text. Revelation is a book for Christians whose spiritual background is Jewish.

THE JUDEO-CHRISTIAN BACKGROUND OF CHERUBIM AND HORSEMEN

For the instructed audience, Rev 6:1–8 would have echoed familiar old pictures from Scripture. For those acquainted with the sacred Hebrew and Christian texts, there were particular areas from which they could draw meaning for what they read in Rev 6:1–8. An important question is how to decide upon the most probable background passages for the images of the living creatures and the four riders. Can a safe methodology be provided in order to walk

---

11. Cf. Rev 8:3–5.

12. Cf. "The angels of God are ascending, bearing the prayers of the needy and distressed to the Father above, and descending, bringing blessing and hope, courage, help, and life, to the children of men." White, *Lift Him Up*, 187.

on the same path the original readers did? For those accustomed to the content of Revelation, Jon Paulien's remarks make sense:

> It is only when the OT background is understood that Revelation can be expected to yield secrets that may have been perfectly plain to the first-century reader. The problem is how to know what OT passage(s) John had in mind when he wrote. *The revelator never cites the OT*; however, he merely alludes to it. The problem of identifying an allusion becomes more complicated when we discover that on many occasions John appears to have quoted loosely from memory, or adapted the OT language to fit his need. It is also quite possible that he used a different text tradition than we have available to us.[13]

Identifying the scriptural places where the allusions come from is paramount for the interpretation.[14] The background indicates the meaning of a word, or passage, in its new context. The process of establishing a direct allusion requires the existence of some parallelism in the text. According to Paulien, there are three kinds of parallels: verbal, thematic, and structural. An allusion becomes possible in proportion to the number of parallels in the text. Our next search is for certain allusions to the four living creatures and the four horsemen in the biblical milieu.

Old Testament Background for the Four Living Creatures

There are two premises which ought to be kept in mind when ascertaining the meaning of the four living creatures in Scripture. The first assumes that there is a historical progression in the use of religious symbols. "In that case, the representations employed at one period must have been so constructed as to convey a fuller

---

13. Paulien, "Interpreting Revelation's Symbolism." Emphasis mine.

14. Paulien states that there are two kinds of references to the Old Testament in Revelation: direct allusions and indirect allusions or echoes. The former guide the researcher toward particular biblical material and are classified as certain, probable, possible, uncertain allusions and non-allusions. The latter do not point the reader or interpreter to a particular background source. Ibid., 90–92.

meaning than those employed at another."[15] What is at first called *cherubim* (Gen 3:24) resembles much of the description of a *seraphim* (Isa 6:1–3). Both are represented in Revelation under the auspices of the living creatures (Rev 4:6–8). The cherubim itself is viewed by Ezekiel as being the living creature from an earlier vision (Ezek 10:20; cf. 1:1–10).

The second consideration is that the diversity shaped by the progression of the symbol does not allow the imposition of a generic meaning based only on a specific representation of it, contradicting all the others. "Progressive differences can only affect what is circumstantial, not what is essential to the subject."[16] Thus what is fundamental in the cherubic imagery must be found in accordance with the whole of the evidence contained in Scripture regarding it, not just with a part.

The cherubim's appearance. "Living creature" is the English for the Greek ζῷον. "In a number of languages the equivalent of 'living things' or 'living creatures' is simply 'those which are alive' or 'those that move about.' ζῷον, therefore, includes essentially quadrupeds, fish, birds, and insects, and is not used in the NT to designate human beings."[17] However, one of the living creatures whom John sees has the face of a man (cf. Rev 4:7). This suggests that the intention of the vision of Revelation is to perceive the four ζῷα as being more than symbols of the animal world.

In the LXX ζῷον stands for the Hebrew חַיָּה. Ezekiel parallels חַיּוֹת (living things) with כְּרוּבִים (cherubim) in Ezek 10:20.[18] In light of the many parallels between the four living creatures in Revelation and Ezekiel, we may conclude that the four ζῷα of Revelation are the celestial beings called in biblical literature

---

15. Fairbairn, *Typology of Scripture*, 216.
16. Ibid.
17. Louw and Nida, *Lexicon of the New Testament*, s.v. "ζῷον."
18. "These were the living creatures I had seen beneath the God of Israel by the Kebar River, and I realized that they were cherubim" (cf. Ezek 1:5).

"cherubim."[19] "From a graphic perspective, the biblical description of cherubim can be divided into two major groups: those that were two-dimensional, as they appeared woven into textiles, or in low relief; and those that were free-standing either as modeled, three-dimensional forms or as living, moving creatures."[20] It seems that in the times of Flavius Josephus no one knew what the Scriptural cherubim looked like. And this makes it unlikely that someone beyond his time could identify a precise profile of them. Speaking of the three-dimensional cherubim of the Temple built by Solomon, Josephus says:

> He also dedicated for the most secret place, whose breadth was twenty cubits, and length the same, two cherubim of solid gold; the height of each of them was five cubits they had each of them two wings stretched out as far as five cubits; wherefore Solomon set them up not far from each other, that with one wing they might touch the southern wall of the secret place, and with another the northern: their other wings, which joined to each other, were a covering to the ark, which was set between them; but *nobody can tell, or even conjecture, what was the shape of these cherubim.*[21]

This definitely strengthens the assumption that the exact nature of the cherubim is not important for the writer of Revelation, or the opposite, that he and his first readers were very much familiar with it, so that he did not consider it crucial to detail it; that is why we should understand the cherubim from the perspective of their symbolic description. Cherubim appear in animal and human pictural language, albeit they are real celestial figures.

---

19. Gen 3:24; Exod 25:18–20; 37:7–9; 1 Sam 4:4; 1 Kgs 6:23, 29, 32, 35; 7:36; 2 Chr 3:7, 10, 14; Pss 18:11; 80:2; 99:1; Isa 37:16; Ezek 10:1–9, 14–16, 18–20; 28:14, 16; 41:18, 20, 25; etc.

20. Meyers, "Cherubim," 117. Those in the first category appeared on the: (1) curtains of the tabernacle (Exod 26:1, 31); (2) veil of the tabernacle (Exod 26:31); (3) veil of the temple (2 Chr 3:14); (4) doors of the temple (1 Kgs 6:32, 35); (5) walls of the temple (2 Chr 3:7).

21. Flavius, *Antichități Iudaice*, 1:440. Emphasis mine.

The four living beings in Rev 6:1–8 are first introduced in Rev 4:6–8. Ezekiel 1 and 10 are passages that seem to speak of the same celestial beings as Rev 6:1–8 (cf. 4:6–8). Strong structural, thematic, and verbal parallels exist between the text of Ezekiel and that of John.

In both Revelation and Ezekiel we find the same four beings, lion, ox, man, and vulture (Ezek 1:10; Rev 4:7). In Ezekiel it is הָרוּחַ (the spirit; τὸ πνεῦμα in LXX) that creates the environment of the four living ones before the throne (Ezek 1:12, 13, 20). He is portrayed with torches (λαμπάδων in LXX; v. 13) and fire (πυρός in LXX; v. 13). In Revelation, "before the throne, seven lamps (λαμπάδες) were blazing (πυρός)" (4:5). Both contexts contain flashes of lighting (ἀστραπαί; Ezek 1:13–14; Rev 4:5). The wheels, which participate in the activity of the four living creatures, being actually an extension of their faces (cf. 1:15–21), were "full of eyes all around (v. 18)." The same is said about the four living creatures of John (Rev 4:6). In both texts there is an expanse above the four living ones and underneath God's throne (Ezek 1:23–26; Rev 4:6). God's glory which encircles Him who was standing on the throne appeared like a rainbow to Ezekiel (Ezek 1:28). John saw the same reality: "A rainbow ... encircled the throne" (Rev 4:3). On account of these evident parallels it is crystal clear that John has Ezek 1 in mind, as background for his material about the four living creatures.

Differences are also part of the textual dynamics. For instance, each of the four living creatures of Ezekiel has four faces (man, lion, ox, and vulture). To John the same beings looked as though they had only one face each. Thus, the four creatures of John sum up the four faces which appear in Ezekiel as features of each creature individually. Another difference concerns the number of wings. Here John changes Ezekiel's report (that the four חַיּוֹת have four wings) by what he sees, namely that each of the four Living Creatures has six wings. The number of wings leads to another Old Testament passage—Isa 6:1–3. However, this last difference opens again the chapter of parallels: Isaiah's seraphim cry to one another "holy, holy, holy" is the Lord (Isa 6:3). This is the refrain of the four cherubim of John, too (Rev 4:8).

Consequently, "the description of Rev 4:6–8 has features reminiscent of both Ezekiel and Isaiah."[22] "John's conception of the ζῷα is clearly composite."[23] On the basis of these numerous links between the appearance of the four living creatures of John with those of Ezekiel and Isaiah we may finally conclude that the four ζῷα of Revelation are cherubim, an angelic order of biblical literature, or, as some prefer to call them, "the highest order of celestial beings."[24] In this case, they are neither cherubim, nor seraphim, but a mixture.

After establishing the background for understanding the four living creatures, the question of the role of the four cherubim in Ezekiel should be asked. John does more than borrow language or imagery, he infers a meaning from Ezekiel. The latter spotted the four living creatures in the midst of fire. The cherubim have special access to God (cf. 28:14, 16) and are bearers of God's throne-chariot. On the tabernacle's Ark of the Covenant there were gold images of cherubim, with outstretched wings, that guarded the mercy seat where the glory of the Lord dwelt (Exod 25:17–22; Num 7:89). God was "enthroned between the cherubim" of the ark of the covenant (1 Sam 4:4; 2 Sam 6:2; Psa 80:1; 99:1; Isa 37:16). This place where God was enthroned was called "the chariot" as Chronicles asserts: "and the weight of the refined gold for the altar of incense. He also gave him the plan for the chariot, that is, the cherubim of gold that spread their wings and shelter the ark of the covenant of the Lord" (1 Chr 28:18).[25] "Since the earthly tabernacle and temple were a copy of the heavenly reality (Heb 8:5), Ezekiel's vision was of the actual throne-chariot of God, borne by cherubim."[26] Thus the cherubim of Ezekiel are the mobile divine throne. This does

---

22. Harris, "Cherub," *Theological Wordbook*, 455.

23. Aune, *Revelation* 1–5, 301.

24. Osborne, *Revelation*, 235.

25. It is interesting that רֶכֶב (chariotry, chariot) or רְכוּב (vehicle, chariot, only in Ps 104:3) is a sort of inverted כרוב (cherub). 25

26. Walvoord and Zuck, *Exposition of the Scriptures*, 1:1228.

not mean that God needs angels to help him move (cf. Ezek 9:3; 10:4, 18). It is just human language; the words are from the military field: God is "carried" in battle.

The wheels from Ezek 1:19–21 suggest locomotion, and "the spirit of the living creatures was in the wheels" (v. 20) may mean the wheels were like an extension of the cherubim on God's throne-chariot. This mobile platform is an indication that the God of Israel is not static. "As He directed the cherubim, the wheels responded and the chariot was propelled on its way."[27]

The concrete significance of God standing on the cherubim-chariot is brilliantly ascertained by Allen:

> The throne vision had already featured in the account of Isaiah's prophetic call in Isa 6. Isaiah saw Yahweh present in judgment, sitting in council, with the verdict of judgment passed and awaiting execution (R. Knierim, *VT* 18 [1968] 54–57; O. H. Stek, *BZ* 16 [1972] 195–97; Long, *JBL* 95 [1976] 361). At an earlier period Micaiah ben Imlah had seen a vision of the enthroned Yahweh in session with his council of judgment, discussing how the death sentence might be carried out (1 Kgs 22:19–22). In line with this tradition, the throne vision that Ezekiel gradually describes functions as a theophany of judgment.[28]

Indeed, this passage is part of a continuing tradition. In Dan 7:9 the wheeled throne has a setting of a divine court of judgment. The text says: "As I looked, thrones were set in place, and the Ancient of Days took his seat. His clothing was as white as snow; the hair of his head was white like wool. His throne was flaming with fire, and its wheels were all ablaze." The next verse announces the beginning of judgment. There seems to be a conscious reminiscence of Ezek 1 in its description of a theophany of judgment upon the kingdoms of the earth.

The scene of the throne room in Rev 4, where the four living creatures are part of the throne (cf. Rev 4:6), suggests the nearness of judgment. And Rev 6:1–8 depicts a series of calamities

---

27. Ibid., 1229.
28. Allen, *Ezekiel 1–19*, 26.

which derive from Christ's work, namely the removing of the seals. However, Rev 6:1–8 does not describe *the* judgment in the technical sense, but only some judgments or afflictions preceding the judgment.

The significance of the four living creatures from Ezekiel to John. One of the first interpretations about the meaning of the four living creatures was delivered by Irenaeus. He "relates the four Gospels to these four faces [of the living creatures], John to the eagle, Luke to the ox, Matthew to the human being and Mark to the lion, pointing respectively to Christ's royalty and deity, to his sacrifice, to his humanity and to his endowment with the Spirit of prophecy."[29] However, this explanation has no textual evidence. Its basis is subjective and rests on the interpreter's imagination.

The four Living Creatures are cherubim, an exalted order of angels frequently associated in Scripture with God's holy power (e.g., 1 Sam 4:4; 2 Sam 6:2; 22:11; Psa 80:1; 99:1; Isa 37:16). After Adam and Eve sinned, God drove them out of Eden and stationed cherubim at the entrance to keep them from returning (Gen 3:24). Two carved cherubim were placed in the Holy of Holies (also called the Most Holy Place), symbolically guarding God's holiness (1 Kgs 6:23–28). Ezekiel speaks about a special cherub using the words: "the anointed cherub who covers"; his duty was to attend God's throne (Ezek 28:14; cf. v. 16).[30]

The "living creatures" in Ezekiel's vision (Ezek 1:5) are four in number, with the general resemblance of a man, but each with four faces and four wings, and straight legs with the feet of an ox. Under their wings are human hands, and these wings are so joined that they are never required to turn. The front face is that of a man; on the sides are the faces of a lion and an ox, while at the back, the face of an eagle. Out of the midst of the faces gleam fire, torches, and lightning; connected with them are four wheels that can turn in every direction, called whirling wheels (Ezek 10:12–13). Like

29. Green, McKnight, and Marshall, *Jesus and the Gospels*, 96.
30. MacArthur, *Revelation 1–11*, 153–54.

the creatures, these wheels are alive and covered with eyes, the sign of intelligence; the spirit of the living creatures is in them.

"The prophet is shown beings he has never beheld before and with which his hearers and readers were unfamiliar. He must describe them in terms understood by men. His feelings of inadequacy are indicated by his frequent use of the term 'likeness.'"[31] The word appears ten times in chapter 1.

The prophetic presentation aimed to encourage the Jews at a time when much of their country lay in ruins through successive invasions and many of the inhabitants were captives in a foreign land. To these oppressed people it appeared that God was no longer in control. The plundering by the heathen nations was interpreted by many as though God no longer cared for them. People failed to see God's hand in the course of history. "They were unaware of the fact that a divine, overruling purpose was at work in the recent developments, as indeed it had been in all ages."[32] The intent of the vision was to instill the idea that as a supreme power God interferes with the earthly rulers and is still in control. This was the overall objective of the vision. Thus, any interpretation must be consistent with this objective.

In Ezekiel's visions about Yahweh's actions in human affairs, the cherub connects humanity with God. "As a guardian of the boundary between the divine and the human and as a mode of transport for the earthly locus of the divine presence, the cherub called forth attentiveness to the transcendent power of YHWH, who burst the bonds of every human concept and construct."[33] God is always above earthly events. He is in charge of history. The living creatures present a picture of God's involvement in history.

White subscribes to this idea regarding the vision of Ezek 1:

> This vision was given to Ezekiel at a time when his mind was filled with gloomy forebodings. He saw the land of his fathers lying desolate. The city that was once full of people was no longer inhabited. The voice of mirth and

---

31. "Ezekiel." *Seventh-day Adventist Bible Commentary*, 4:576.
32. Ibid., 576–77.
33. Launderville, "Ezekiel's Cherub," 182.

the song of praise were no more heard within her walls. The prophet himself was a stranger in a strange land, where boundless ambition and savage cruelty reigned supreme. That which he saw and heard of human tyranny and wrong distressed his soul, and he mourned bitterly day and night. But the wonderful symbols presented before him beside the river Chebar revealed an overruling power mightier than that of earthly rulers. Above the proud and cruel monarchs of Assyria and Babylon the God of mercy and truth was enthroned. The wheellike complications that appeared to the prophet to be involved in such confusion were under the guidance of an infinite hand. The Spirit of God, revealed to him as moving and directing these wheels, brought harmony out of confusion; so the whole world was under His control. Myriads of glorified beings were ready at His word to overrule the power and policy of evil men, and bring good to His faithful ones.[34]

God's people should find faith even in the most puzzling circumstances. The four living creatures of Revelation as a whole thus express the idea of powerful divine providence. They represent "angelic beings that are used by the Creator in executing his rule and his divine will in all the orders of his creation. They are created spirits who are thought of as mediating the divine energy and power in all the world."[35] It is important to remember that the book of Revelation is addressed primarily to the Christians of the first century; thus it becomes significant and paramount that God's almighty providence, conveyed by the four ζῷα, gives the tone of God's implication in human history until the end. His involvement is shown by controlling the deliverance of the four riders of the first four seals, thus proving that God is ruler to the end.

"To the churches about to enter a period of severe testing and persecution a declaration of God's unlimited might would bring strength and encouragement."[36] This assurance of God's control

---

34. White, *Testimonies*, 751.
35. Ladd, *Revelation of John*, 77.
36. Mounce, *Book of Revelation*, 139.

would not have to be perceived as a promise of avoiding any trouble. God's servants are often severely tested, but protected (cf. Dan 6:22). "The faces of the cherub in Ezekiel—that of a human, a lion, an ox, and an eagle (1:1; 10:14)—testify to the powerful, often conflicting forces that come together in human experience."[37] In Revelation, the four cherubim compound different facets of divine *providentia*. Basically, this means that their activity consists of both "giving glory" to God through their constant song (cf. Rev 4:8), and praising Him through their actions in the human field.

Dale Launderville notes the interesting movement of God in Ezekiel through His cherubim: "The four cherubim of the throne chariot played a key role in coordinating the movement of the chariot that conveyed YHWH from the Jerusalem temple to the exiles in Babylon (Ezek 1:4–28; 10:1–22) and then to the ideal reconstructed temple of Ezek 43:1–5."[38] Accordingly, divine superintendence is concerned with the Israelites dispersed in Babylon. God declares through Ezekiel: "Although I sent them far away among the nations and scattered them among the countries, yet for a little while I have been a sanctuary for them in the countries where they have gone" (Ezek 11:16). Not only has He moved towards Israel to create a living temple around them, but also the exiles were to follow God's glory into the new reconstructed temple (Ezek 43:1–5; cf. 43:7). We see again that the four cherubim carry the presence of God among His people in order to lead them to an ideal future in the presence of God. This echoes the Old Testament Ark of the Covenant which was carried by four men with a similar purpose. According to Num 10:33 "the ark of the covenant of the Lord went before them [the Israelites in the wilderness] ... to find them a place to rest." It seem that this was one of the ark's permanent roles (cf. Deut 1:33).

Revelation has its own Babylon and Israelites dispersed within it (cf. Rev 18:1–4). God's providence looks over them with much interest. The activity of the four cherubim seeks to determine the exiles to depart from the spiritual eschatological Babylon. This

37. Launderville, "Ezekiel's Cherub," 169.
38. Ibid., 174.

will be accomplished through judgmental actions. "Both Ezekiel's description and that in Revelation 4 describe what could be called the divine war machine ready to unleash judgment."[39] The four living creatures are God's superintendents who act from the preliminary phases in Rev 6 to the final call of the mighty angel of Rev 18. So, God is manifested to the exiles through the cherubim's actions. The final phase of His movable presence is that of the new temple, namely the New Jerusalem.

Old Testament Background for the Four Riders

Horses, riders, and chariots of Zechariah. The image of the four riders is drawn particularly from Zechariah's material. "It is, of course, obvious to all expositors that the vision of the four horsemen in the Apocalypse immediately suggests the visions of Zechariah 1:7-11 and Zechariah 6:1-8. It is clear that, despite considerable differences in detail, the material of Revelation 6:1-8 finds its true Scriptural prototype in these Old Testament passages."[40]

This book was written towards the end of the Babylonian captivity (Zech 1:12). The introductory vision reveals God's love for Jerusalem while the holy city is still to be recovered. The vision is built upon symbols. In the first scene the angel of the Lord, who appears to the prophet as a "man riding a red horse" (Zech 1:8; cf. v. 10-11), is standing among myrtle trees in a ravine. Behind him are other red, brown, and white horses. A burdensome question is raised by the angel of the Lord: "Lord Almighty, how long will you withhold mercy from Jerusalem and from the towns of Judah, which you have been angry with these seventy years?" (1:12). The same question will be addressed in Revelation by the martyrs of the fifth seal (Rev 6:10). They are eager for God's intervention.

In both books God's response is guaranteed but delayed (Zech 1:14-21; Rev 6:11). He works in His time. He also uses horses as instruments (in Zechariah's book the symbol of horses

---

39. MacArthur, *Revelation 1–11*, 153.
40. Hodges, "First Horseman of the Apocalypse," 325.

is conjoined with chariots). What is communicated in the symbol of horses? It is likely that the image of horses in Zechariah had its background in the postal system first introduced in Persia.[41] Horses were used to send messages. In the beginning, the system was in the king's custody. The riders delivered only correspondence from the royal court. Thus, "the ones the Lord has sent to go throughout the earth" (Zech 1:10) represent his mounted couriers (cf. Esth 8:8, 10) by whom he answers the petitions of his people (cf. Zech 1:12). Each of their actions is a message from God.

Zechariah is equally interested in the meaning of the horses. The answer he received is that these "are the ones the Lord has sent to go throughout the earth" (Zech 1:10; cf. v. 11). Although the statement is not completely clear, we can assume that these are not ordinary horses. This assumption is postulated on two things: first, the horses run in a worldwide campaign, and second, these animals (or their riders) have the ability to talk to God (1:11; 6:7). It is not possible to see these horses as simple animals. Their activity transcends a local sphere. They run all over the world. They cover the entire planet and, after finishing their mission, they report to the Sovereign. They also cannot be just a dim symbol of "divine judicial power exerted in judgment, carrying out the purposes of

---

41. Deriving information from Herodotus, it is now taught that the postal service in the world to ever operate on a regular basis was established in the 6th century BC, in ancient Iran, during Cyrus the Great (550 BC–529 BC). The service used the system of either a messenger, or relay messengers. The messengers were riding horses and carrying mail by day and night; the stations were placed to such distance from each other that a horse needed no resting or feeding, but could run ceaselessly. The riders would take stops at Post Houses regularly displaced on the way, in order to either get a rested horse or to pass on their transportations to another messenger for the remaining distance. The system is alluded to in the book of Esth 8:8, 10. Herodotus describes the system in these words: "It is said that as many days as there are in the whole journey, so many are the men and horses that stand along the road, each horse and man at the interval of a day's journey. These are stopped neither by snow nor rain nor heat nor darkness from accomplishing their appointed course with all speed. The first rider delivers his charge to the second, the second to the third, and thence it passes on from hand to hand, even as in the Greek torch-bearers' race in honor of Hephaestus." Herodotus, *Histories*, 96–97.

God."⁴² They are not impersonal forces or phenomena, because they communicate with God (cf. Zech 1:11).

Something probably relevant is found in Job 1:7. When attending a heavenly meeting Satan was asked where he came from. His answer was "from roaming through the earth and going back and forth in it." This is essentially the same trajectory of the horses in Zechariah. "When the powerful horses went out, they were straining to go throughout the earth. And he said, 'Go throughout the earth!' So they went throughout the earth" (Zech 6:7). The difference is that the horses are sent by the Lord, while Satan has his particular purpose for this activity. It appears that such an enterprise is not human, but rather angelic.

This hypothesis is supported by Zech 6:1–8. The prophet sees four chariots led by four different groups of horses, each group having a different color. The prophet asks the same question: What do the horses stand for? The answer is given in Zech 6:5, which reads: "אֵלֶּה אַרְבַּע רֻחוֹת הַשָּׁמַיִם יוֹצְאוֹת מֵהִתְיַצֵּב עַל־אֲדוֹן כָּל־הָאָרֶץ," "These are the four spirits of heaven, going out from standing in the presence of the Lord of the whole world." The word "spirit" is the English term for רוּחַ (wind, breath, spirit). Even the literal translation "the four winds" underlines the same idea that the four groups of horses are divine agencies, spirits, or angels.

"To regard the winds exclusively as symbols of God's judgments is to emphasize only a part of the truth."⁴³ Throughout the Old Testament, in the presence of the Lord heavenly hosts (Job 1:6; 2:1) are seen. In 1 Kings 22:19 God is shown sitting on His throne, with all the host of heaven standing beside Him on His right hand and on His left. Daniel 7:10 emphasizes that God is encircled by a judicial court compound by thousands who "stood before him." This is in total agreement with the NT. The angel who appeared to Zechariah with a message about the birth of John the Baptist announced: "I am Gabriel, who stands in the presence of God," as Luke wrote (Luke 1:19). Based on similar arguments, Unger's conclusion is that "there is every reason to believe these chariots

---

42. Feinberg, "Exegetical Studies in Zechariah," 170.
43. Leupold, *Exposition of Zechariah*, 115.

represent 'personal beings,' that is, angelic messengers rather than impersonal forces."[44]

God "makes winds his messengers" (Psa 104:4). This is a poetic metaphor. We should not exaggerate its meaning. The word "wind" is the same for רוּחַ, here with a literal sense. Yet, the association of angels and winds is evident. The author of Hebrews applies Psa 104:4 to angels in Heb 1:7. Zechariah 6:5 affirms that they stand "in the presence of the Lord." In Rev 5:11 we find that in the throne room, encircling the throne there are "many angels, numbering thousands upon thousands, and ten thousand times ten thousand" (cf. Psa 68:17—angels compound God's chariots). Thus, angels is the "the simplest and more natural explanation"[45] of the four winds in Zechariah. They are "ministering spirits sent to serve those who will inherit salvation" (Heb 1:14).

With respect to the horses, it is very meaningful that Rev 6:1–8 displays the horses before revealing their riders. It appears that in Revelation the horse is important alone. In Zechariah there is another sense of the horse picture. In Zech 10:3 God says: "My anger burns against the shepherds, and I will punish the leaders; for the Lord Almighty will care for his flock, the house of Judah, and make them like a proud horse in battle." Very significantly, one of Judah's weapons was "the battle bow" (v. 4), recalling Rev 6:2. Thus, the horse may symbolize God's people in battle. The relationship with the angels is that the angelic beings accompany the church in its battles.

Old Testament pictures of angels. The angels are symbolized in the Hebrew testament by winds, horses, horsemen, and chariots. In the Old Testament the expression "four winds" has two basic meanings. The first one refers to the four points of the compass (1 Chr 9:24; Jer 49:36; Ezek 37:9; Dan 8:8; 11:4; Zech 2:6; Matt 24:31; Mark 13:27). The second meaning is that of angels which, to a certain extent, is a meaning hidden in symbolism and diffused.

---

44. Unger, *Zechariah*, 104.
45. Baron, *Visions and Prophecies*, 175.

For instance, in Jer 49:36 God threatens Elam saying: "I will bring against Elam the four winds from the four quarters of the heavens; I will scatter them to the four winds, and there will not be a nation where Elam's exiles do not go." "The four winds" appears to be the destination of Elam's judgment, showing that it will be scattered all over the world, or in every direction of the compass. But it also conveys the instruments of judgment. "The winds" will "blow" against Elam. The winds become the instruments of judgment. The reference to wind here can hardly be understood as common, physical wind. "The wind is the most appropriate among all earthly things for symbolizing the Spirit of God, or the energy of the divine operation; cf. Zech. 6:5, Dan. 7:2."[46] This is rather a metaphorical expression. Beyond the metaphor, we may assume that "the four winds" or the angels, who stand "in the presence of the Lord," are involved in human affairs. They accomplish the divine will in a certain context. Definitely, there were historical powers that conquered Elam, but they succeeded by the instrumentality of God's angels. Angels leading the destiny of nations and kingdoms are a revealed fact in the book of Daniel (Dan 10:13, 21; cf. 2:21).

Scripture depicts the action of the wind during some very important moments of biblical history. Winds cause the cessation of the flood (Gen 8:1); they are responsible for bringing some of the plagues on Egypt (Exod 10:13); for parting the Red Sea and for closing it on the Egyptians (Exod 14:21; 15:10); and also bringing the quails to Israel in the desert (Num 11:31). This does not mean that in Scripture the winds are univocally angels, but it is very probable that angels are present in various phenomena that contain the action of natural winds. For instance, the wind that brought the quails in the desert was a real wind, but it "went out from the Lord" (Num 11:31); it might have been caused by the angels who are "going out from standing in the presence of the Lord" (Zech 6:5). The instruments by which God accomplishes his will are the angels (Heb 1:14). Their involvement in those incidents has to be regarded as bringing the winds. Thus, the winds are not superseded by angels, but mingle with them in the phenomenon.

---

46. Keil and Delitzsch, *Zechariah*, 418.

Angels and Beasts

In the Old Testament it is not unusual to find angels symbolized by winds, horses, horsemen, and chariots. This is evident from the following examples. Sounds of marching are heard when the Lord accompanies David's army in battle (2 Sam 5:24; 1 Chr 14:15). The Lord is also represented by His hosts of angels. When Elijah goes up to heaven the Bible describes the event in these words: "As they were walking along and talking together, suddenly a chariot of fire and horses of fire appeared and separated the two of them, and Elijah went up to heaven in a whirlwind" (2 Kgs 2:11). Again, a chariot and horses are present to fulfill God's plan for His servant.

Another example is when Elisha and his servant are surrounded by the Syrian army. The prophet prays to God to comfort his frightened companion. "Then the Lord opened the servant's eyes, and he looked and saw the hills full of horses and chariots of fire all around Elisha" (2 Kgs 6:17). When Isaiah describes God's acts of judgment by which He will deliver His people and punish His enemies, he says: "See, the Lord is coming with fire, and his chariots are like a whirlwind; he will bring down his anger with fury, and his rebuke with flames of fire" (Isa 66:15). One other instance where horses and chariots are mentioned is found in Hab 3:8, "Were you angry with the rivers, O Lord? Was your wrath against the streams? Did you rage against the sea when you rode with your horses and your victorious chariots?" In conclusion, the picture of horses and chariots of God suggests divine intervention through His serving angels. They represent His army.

Another significant passage for this topic is Ezek 1:24. Describing the four living creatures in detail, Ezekiel says that the sound of their wings moving is "like the tumult of an army." It is also interesting that the first element in the vision of Ezek 1 is the wind (Ezek 1:4). Before seeing the four living creatures, Ezekiel beholds a tempest (סְעָרָה - storm wind). This, along with clouds, fire, and light, compounds the display of the living creatures. The audition, as well as the visualization of angels in the symbols of horses, riders and chariots, communicates the idea of an army.

The relationship between the four cherubim and the four beasts of Daniel 7. Another metaphorical usage of the "four winds" is found in Dan 7:2. Daniel says: "In my vision at night I looked, and there before me were the four winds of heaven churning up the great sea." Here the wind is definitely a token of angels' activity. The agitation of the sea brings four different empires on the scene. This indicates that angels are involved in shaping history. The conclusion also fits perfectly with Dan 2:21: "He changes times and seasons; he sets up kings and deposes them." God changes kings through his mighty messengers, as Dan 10:13, 20 points to.

Florin Lăiu suggests an interesting comparison between the four great beasts (living creatures) of Dan 7:3 and the four living creatures of Ezek 1:5. Both groups are comprised of four beings. Other similarities refer to: zoologic and anthropologic composites; to God who is in both cases above the creatures as universal King and Judge; to the throne and fire (Ezek 1: 26–27; Dan 7:9–10); and to the expression "son of man" (Ezek 2:1; Dan 7:13). Finally, there is a partial animal correspondence: Lion (the first beast), eagle (the first beast), man (the first beast and the little horn of the fourth beast) eyes. The calf (cherub), as the most valuable sacrifice, has no correspondence in the four ferocious beasts of Daniel, and it may correspond to the persecuted "saints of the Most High." Lăiu concludes that the beasts of Daniel's vision are a parody of the four cherubim, rather than an interpretation. They are rebel "cherubim," who no longer carry Yahweh's *merkabah*.[47] They are an evil replica of the four cherubim and come as a reaction to the winds blowing upon the great sea.

Relationship between the four riders of Revelation 6:1–8 and the four angels of Revelation 7:1–3 and 9:13–16. Generally, the image of the "four riders" in Rev 6:1–8 should be interpreted as a symbol of a universal campaign of God's angels for bringing divine judgment (cf. Zech 6:8). Both contexts "indicate that these are connected with

---

47. Lăiu, "Exegetical Study of Daniel 7–9," 55.

the execution of divine judgments."[48] It is a universal campaign indicated by their number that fits the four corners of the earth. However, each of the four horsemen in Rev 6:1–8 hits only a part of the earth. Obviously, in Revelation there is a progression of divine judgment. There is a direct relationship between the four riders in Rev 6:1–8 and the four angels in Rev 7:1–3 and the same group in Rev 9:13–16. Table 1 highlights the links between the three passages.

What is the relationship between the four riders and the four angels of Rev 7:1–3? Revelation 7:1 says, "After this I saw four angels standing at the four corners of the earth, holding back the four winds of the earth to prevent any wind from blowing on the land or on the sea or on any tree." The text uses the same language. Four mighty angels are to restrain the activity of the "four winds of the earth." These winds are destructive. The main difference between the judgments brought by the horses in Rev 6 and the judgments brought by the winds in Rev 7 is that the former hits the earth partially, while the latter brings total destruction.

Carson believes that "*the four angels . . . holding back the four winds of the earth* are an alternative symbol of the four horsemen of the previous chapter (so in Zech 6:5). The destructive fury of the winds represents the whole manifestation of judgment symbolized by the seals, trumpets and cups of wrath."[49] There are scholars who suggest that based on Zech 6:5 the four winds of Rev 7 might be interpreted as another depiction of the four horsemen of Rev 6.[50] Apparently, the parallel between the four horsemen in Rev 6 and the four winds in Rev 7 compels us to identify the four angels who restrict the winds with the four living creatures that hold the four riders to their command.

However, there are also some significant differences. First of all, while the four riders are summoned to "go" (Rev 6:1, 3, 5, 7), the four winds are restrained completely in their destructive

---

48. Vine, Unger, and White, *Dictionary of Old and New Testament Words*, "Wind," 677.

49. Carson, *Revelation*.

50. E.g., Mounce, *Book of Revelation*, 165.

activity (Rev 7:2-3). Then, the judgments of the four riders are limited, while the "blowing" of the four winds of the earth is complete (note the expression "on the earth, nor on the sea, nor on any tree" in v. 1). The last distinction consists of the fact that if the four horsemen are one and the same thing with the four winds, it is necessary to interpret the first rider in the negative sense, since all of the four winds are destructive. However, the first rider has a positive aspect, which will be developed later.

Consequently, the four riders (Rev 6) are not one and the same thing with the four winds (Rev 7). It follows then that the living creatures (Rev 6) do not correspond with the four angels (Rev 7). In this paper I suggest that the four living creatures deliver the four riders, that is, the cherubim in the near proximity of the divine throne direct God's army (or part of it) formed by angels. These "soldiers" do their work of partial judgment. At the last stage of human history, just before the sealing of God's people, the four riders, or the four angels (in Rev 7), hold the destructive winds that represent the total and final evil destruction.

The four angels in Rev 7 are actually the four riders in the last phase of their ministry. They hold the four winds of the earth, which symbolize the earthly forces that will mingle in the final destruction. Behind these "earthly" winds might be some "heavenly" beings, or evil spirits.

This is supported by the close association between the four angels in Rev 7:1-3 and the four angels in Rev 9:13-16. It seems that the two groups are one and the same. Thus, the destructive winds restrained by the four angels in Rev 7:1-3 are linked to, presumably, the demonic forces described in the scene of the sixth trumpet under the image of a mounted army.

Table 1. Four Riders and Four Angels

	Rev 6:1–8	Rev 7:1–3	Rev 9:13–16
Characters	Four horse-rider teams under the command of four cherubim	Four angels under the command of another angel "coming up from the east" (v. 2)	Four angels under the command of the sixth angel with trumpet
Location	To and fro on the earth	At the four corners of the earth	At the great river Euphrates
Characteristics	Permission to harm and kill 25% of humanity	Permission to harm everything except the sealed after the sealing of God's people	Permission to harm and kill one third of humanity
Mission	Harm and kill	Hold the four winds of earth until the sealing of God's servants. Implies that after the sealing, they will release the four winds, and the latter are actually harming	Leaving Euphrates means that Babylon is in danger. They will no more guard the city. This means that those who will kill one third of humanity are not the angels, but those whom the angels will no more reject
Target	God's people and God's enemy	The land, the sea and the trees (symbol of people), in the context, the unsealed	A third of mankind
Purpose	To correct in order to return to God	To punish; it is too late to return to God	To correct in order to return to God

What Revelation reveals is that there is a war between good and evil on the level of angels, and on the human level—between the church and Babylon. The two armies will collide in the end, and while loyal angels protect the sealed, evil angels will assail the unsealed. The conflict will grow in intensity under the control of the four cherubim. When God's people are prepared spiritually, the evil winds will blow upon the whole earth. But then the saints will be under divine shelter.

THE OLD TESTAMENT BACKGROUND OF THE SEVEN SEALS

Curses against God's People

After God redeemed Israel from their Egyptian bondage, He made a covenant with them that primarily asked for holiness. Leviticus 11:44 says: "Be holy, because I am holy." Because of the sanctity of God, His people had to be a nation of saints. God's final people are also called "saints" and called to holiness by obedience to the Law (Rev 14:12). If the Israelites obeyed and acted in conjunction with God, they would receive rewards and blessings. In contrast, if Israel was unable to achieve this, her continual disobedience would call, as a consequence, the curses of the covenant to fall upon them.[51] It is interesting to observe along with Jon Paulien and others[52] that the language of Rev 6:1-8 consistently parallels the covenant curses in the Pentateuch that were executed in the Babylonian exile.

These curses of the covenant are described in the Old Testament in terms of "war, famine, pestilence, and wild beasts." A list of similar judgments is found in the Sibylline Oracles,[53] but John most probably recalls backgrounds such as Ezek 14:21, which speaks about the "four severe judgments" (Ezek 14:21). Another basic biblical reference with regard to these curses is Lev 26:21-26:

> If you remain hostile toward me and refuse to listen to me, I will multiply your afflictions seven times over, as your sins deserve. I will send *wild animals* against you, and they will rob you of your children, destroy your

---

51. E.g., Deut 28:15-68; Moses urged Israel before his death to remain faithful to God; otherwise the blessings would be replaced with curses.

52. Paulien, "Seven Seals," 222-24. Cf. Beale, *Book of Revelation*, 372-74.

53. Keener, *Background Commentary*.

cattle and make you so few in number that your roads will be deserted. If in spite of these things you do not accept my correction but continue to be hostile toward me, I myself will be hostile toward you and will afflict you for your sins seven times over. And I will bring the *sword* upon you to avenge the breaking of the covenant. When you withdraw into your cities, I will send a *plague* among you, and you will be given into enemy hands. When I cut off your supply of bread, ten women will be able to bake your bread in one oven, and they will dole out the bread by weight. You will eat, but you will not be satisfied.

The four afflictions are penalties that God would send upon His people Israel because of her disloyalty.[54] They "are rooted in God's promise to punish apostasy to Israel in general (Lev 26:22–23) and in Jerusalem in particular (Ezek 5; 33:37)."[55] These curses directed towards Israel are reiterated symbolically in God's people's case over the Christian era. The parallels are indicated in table 2.

Whenever God's people are unfaithful, consequences will follow. Table 2 makes it easier to visualize that the four calamities are comprised in the last three of the first four seals (cf. Rev 6:4–8). Moreover, the fourth one is an intensification of the two previous

Table 2. The Four Divine Penalties

Leviticus	Revelation
Wild beasts (Lev 26:22)	Wild beasts of the earth (Rev 6:8)
Sword (Lev 26:25)	A large sword (Rev 6:4, 8)
Plague (Lev 26:25)	Plague (Rev 6:8)
Bread by weight (Lev 26:26)	A pair of scales to weigh wheat and barley (Rev 6:5, 6, 8)

seals in accordance with the "seven times over" expression of Leviticus which is systematically repeated. The sword of the second

---

54. Eugene Boring sees the four horsemen as futuristic judgments, the target being more general: "The four horsemen portray the judgment of God on human arrogance and rebellion." Boring, *Revelation*, 119. However, the parallels with the OT make his identification too general.

55. Malina, *Stat Visions and Sky Journeys*, 126.

mark and the famine of the third one are repeated in the fourth mark, which adds and thus intensifies the results of disobedience, the plague, and the wild beasts. Even more, the wild beasts appear further in chapter 13.

Either the Israelites' feeble faith in Jesus or their superficial and outward keeping of God's commandments unleashes the four banes; there are four categories of divine penalties. Sometimes they are fulfilled literally[56] in the history of the Hebrew people. The covenant curses, in the initial phase, are preliminary judgments of God on His people with a very clear purpose: to awake the apostate people and lead them to repentance and a renewed relationship with God (cf. Lev 26:18, 21, 23, and 27).

Curses against God's Enemies

Most of God's judgments upon His people consisted in foreign oppression. Assyrian, Babylonian, Medo-Persian, or other alien swords banished peace, bread, health, and security from Israel's land. The same language and concepts of Lev 26 are repeated by Moses in his discourse in Deut 32. Verses 23–25 state: "I will heap calamities upon them and spend my arrows[57] against them. I will send wasting *famine* against them, consuming pestilence and *deadly plague*; I will send against them the fangs of *wild beasts*, the venom of vipers that glide in the dust. In the street the *sword* will make them childless; in their homes terror will reign. Young men

56. Of particular interest here would be a quotation of Dio Cassius which David Aune included in his commentary with reference to the causalities the Jews endured during the Bar-Kohba revolt (A.D. 132–135): "Five hundred and eighty thousand men were slain in the various raids and battles [i.e., the *sword*], and the number of those that perished by *famine, disease* and fire was past finding out. Thus nearly the whole of Judaea was made desolate, a result of which the people had had forewarning before the war. For the tomb of Solomon, which the Jews regard as an object of veneration, fell to pieces of itself and collapsed, and many *wolves and hyenas* rushed howling into their cities." Aune, *Revelation 6–16*, 402.

57. The word "arrows" appears to have a direct relationship to the first seal. Yet, in Deut 32 the arrows represent all of God's weapons, detailed afterwards in the passage.

and young women will perish, infants and gray-haired men" (emphasis mine). The new element of Deut 32 is that this desolation is the work of the צָרֵימ (adversaries, foes; cf. Deut 32:37) which receive permission from God to be a burden for His ungodly people.

However, YHWH is concerned that these foes could boast, saying: "Our hand has triumphed; the Lord has not done all this" (Deut 32:27). Divine providence should deal even more strongly with the enemy. Deuteronomy 32:41–43 vividly depicts "the sword" being crushed by God's sword. This means that the strangers who disciplined Israel would also be disciplined. Does God punish a person or country that is sent to chasten His people for unfaithfulness? Yes, but for a very clear reason. Some of Zechariah's visions are particularly instructive to this issue.

In the first chapter of Zechariah the prophet saw in vision four different colored horses as agents of divine judgment. Comfortingly and kindly, God answered the question, "How long will you withhold mercy from Jerusalem and from the towns of Judah, which you have been angry with these seventy years?" (1:12). The seventy years of the captivity, prophesied by Jeremiah (25:11–12; 29:10), were on the eve of their conclusion at the time of Daniel's great prayer of intercession of Dan 9; they ended with the capture of Babylon, and the edict of Cyrus, permitting the Jews to return to their homeland (2 Chr 36:22–23; Ezra 1:1). The angel facilitating the vision proclaims not only Israel's restoration but also God's feelings toward the oppressors: "Then the angel who was speaking to me said, 'Proclaim this word: This is what the Lord Almighty says: «I am very jealous for Jerusalem and Zion, but I am very angry with the nations that feel secure. I was only a little angry, but they added to the calamity»'" (Zech 1:14–15). The concept of addition, or help—as עָזַר primarily means—exposes the oppressors as overdoing the discipline. God never intended the quantity of distress Israel experienced from her enemies. He is not represented by the amount of suffering Israel was led to. Those foes overacted their role, so God turned against them. This dimension of God's revenge for His people, as part of the covenant, is the essence of the fifth seal (cf. Rev 6:10) which contains the "how long?" question reminiscent of Zech 1:12.

God's judgments follow a progression. They scourge His people first (cf. Ezek 9:1–7; 1 Pet 4:17) with one single purpose, namely to prepare and seal a kingdom of saints. Second, the divine wrath will blow upon the enemy because they overdid their corrective role. The sixth seal reveals the coming of Jesus, which is a judgment in itself. God's people are rescued while His enemies experience severe and devastating hits of retribution, portrayed in the scene of the blowing of the seven trumpets. Revelation 8–9 prepares the final and ultimate phase of judgment described in Rev 16–20. In conclusion, from the Old Testament perspective, the first four seals cannot just signify "various forms of injustice on earth,"[58] but they outline the covenant curses as a result of unfaithfulness to the message of salvation. By using punishment, God intends to spiritually awaken and remotivate His people.

THE NEW TESTAMENT BACKGROUND OF REVELATION 6:1–8

As Jesus might be considered the ultimate author of Revelation,[59] the vision of Rev 6 could be compared with Jesus' eschatological discourse on the Mount of Olives (Matt 24, Mark 13, and Luke 21). "It is likely to have in Matt 24 the key of Revelation."[60] In His

58. So Herms, *An Apocalypse for the Church*, 217–18.

59. The phrase "Ἀποκάλυψις Ἰησοῦ Χριστοῦ" might refer linguistically to Christ either as subject or object. It might either mean that Christ is the object revealed in this book, and that its great purpose is to make Him known; or it may mean that this is a revelation which Christ makes to mankind, that is, it is His in the sense that He communicates it to the world. "Hort takes it as objective genitive (revelation about Jesus Christ), but Swete rightly argues for the subjective genitive because of the next clause." Robertson, *Revelation of John*. For the above reasons, one could conclude that Christ is in a sense the author of the Apocalypse, although He might also be considered the One Revealed.

60. Lăiu, *Daniel & Apocalipsa*, 70. As R. H. Charles also suggests: "The more closely we study the Seals in connection with Mark 13, Matt 24, Luke 21, the more strongly we shall be convinced that our author finds his chief and controlling authority in the eschatological scheme there set forth." Charles,

end-times sermon, Christ describes the events that will occur at the time of the end. The language in Rev 6 echoes pictures found in the Synoptic Apocalypse. There are many convincing verbal and thematic parallels between the two, which make the comparison valid.

A perusal of the passages mentioned above emphasizes the conclusion. Almost all of the elements appear in at least two instances. Stefanović created a table paralleling the following items: the gospel spreading (Rev 6:1–2–Matt 24:14; Mark 13:10), war (Rev 6:3–4–Matt 24:6–7; Mark 13:7–8; Luke 21:9–10), famine (Rev 6:5–6–Matt 24:7; Mark 13:8; Luke 21:11), pestilence (Rev 6:7–8–Luke 21:11), persecution (Rev 6:9–11–Matt 24:9–10; Mark 13:9–13; Luke 21:12–17), heavenly signs (Rev 6:12–13–Matt 24:29; Mark 13:24–25; Luke 21:25–26), tribes mourn (Rev 6:15–17–Matt 24:30), and the second coming (Rev 6:17–Matt 24:30; Mark 13:26; Luke 21:27).[61]

The period of time that Jesus envisions in His speech stretches from His ascension to the time prior to the second coming. The Old Testament milieu of the covenant with its blessings and curses is the foundation of Christ's language and motifs for the end time. "The parallels between the Synoptic Apocalypse and Revelation 6 indicate that the scene of the opening of the seven seals refers to the events taking place on earth from the time of Christ's exaltation on the heavenly throne until his return to earth."[62] Although the first-century Christians believed they were living during the time of the end–because of the presence of wars, famines, pestilence, persecution of the faithful, false prophets, the preaching of the Gospel, etc.–the intention of John's text extends beyond the first century, up to the end of history.

Commentary on the Revelation of St John, 1:158.

61. Stefanović, *Revelation*, 220.

62. Ibid.

CHAPTER 3

The Four Living Creatures as Individuals

IN THE APOCALYPSE THE four living creatures appear either together, entering different scenes one by one (e.g., Rev 6:1–8); individually, playing specific roles in certain circumstances (e.g., Rev 15:7); or as a unit (e.g., Rev 4–5; 7:11; 14:3; 19:4). When they appear as a unit, the reader picks up their general significance. The way they are first introduced in Revelation[1] brings to John's view a sea of glass which evokes the cosmic dimension of the panorama. The image of the throne set above the waters proclaims the power of God over the material elements. "The Apocalypse here represents God as the Creator."[2] The book of Genesis describes creation in terms of a victory over the waters. The theme appears also in Psa 104:3 when we read, "and lays the beams of his upper chambers on their waters," signifying that God is sovereign over creation. In relation to God, who is presented as Creator, the four cherubim

---

1. Revelation 4:6: "Also before the throne there was what looked like a sea of glass, clear as crystal. In the center, around the throne, were four living creatures, and they were covered with eyes, in front and in back."

2. Doukhan, *Secrets of Revelation*, 53.

stand for creation as a whole.³ The four ζῷα praise God as representatives of the creation.

Apparently, they are not a symbol of the universal creation. They are only the terrestrial creation in miniature. They cannot represent the earthly creation in its present disordered state. Naturally, a lion, a calf, a man, and a vulture cannot associate. The cherubim are a picture of an ideal creation. As Beale puts it, Rev 4:8 depicts "the worship of an ideal community."⁴ Isaiah catches several glimpses of this future community. According to him, after the time when the Root (LXX—ῥίζα) of David will arise and judge (Isa 11:1–5), things will be reshaped on the earth. One of the biggest changes is that a little child will lead a lion and a calf together in the pasture (Isa 11:6). What is now antagonistic will then be at peace. Presently not everyone recognizes God as Creator, the only one worthy of praise and worship. The cherubim do, in advance, what the renewed creation will do.

The function of these four living ones is to guard and worship God, and at certain times execute His judgments. "They are a special order of creation, created for a specific purpose in God's presence. The living ones have access to God, even to the point of having entré into the midst of His throne."⁵ Although they are angelic beings, they typify the totality of creation. The way they are pictured suggests nothing about their nature.⁶ We cannot assume

---

3. About the four living creatures Doukhan paraphrases an ancient Jewish story, a midrash, which uses the same language. According to it, Rabbi Abahu, its author, says that there are four powerful creatures: the eagle, the most powerful among the birds; the ox, the most powerful among domesticated animals; the lion, the most powerful among wild animals; and man, the most powerful among all animals (ibid., 54). So, while the 24 elders stand for the ransomed humanity, the four living creatures represent the whole of creation.

4. Beale, *Book of Revelation*, 331.

5. Mills, *Revelation*.

6. With reference to the fourth Living Creature the Greek text that ἔχων τὸ πρόσωπον ὡς ἀνθρώπου, "has the face of a human" (Rev 4:7). David Aune believes that this phrase "disturbs the careful symmetry and stereotypical phraseology of the descriptions of the first, second, and fourth creatures. Instead, we would have expected the phrase to read ὅμοιον προσώπῳ ἀνθρώπου, "like a human face." Aune, *Revelation 1–5*, 299. It was important to clarify when the

The Four Living Creatures as Individuals

that the exact constitution of the cherubim is partly human and partly animal. They are angels and man is inferior to angels, while animal is inferior to man. They are pictured in this way to signify something. The purpose of this chapter is to discover the meaning of their animal and human depiction.

Patrick Fairbairn's typological approach is helpful to delineate here, although it differs from the approach of this study. He helpfully states that the cherubim are special agents of God's created world which represent humanity united in diversity[7] and accomplish an interim assignment. This interregnum consists of leading fallen humanity back to its privileged state. In a sense, says Fairbairn, they (the cherubim) hold that high position of living in God's very presence in an intimate spiritual relationship. They are in symbol what the redeemed mankind will become in reality. Therefore, he states, when humankind will achieve the privileged state of the cherubim, the symbol is laid aside. There is no need for it anymore. In Fairbairn's words, the cherubim "have fulfilled their temporary existence; and when no longer needed, they vanish like the guiding stars of night before the bright sunshine of eternal day."[8]

By this, Fairbairn cannot suggest that the cherubim will cease to exist as such. In this direction we find many conjectures. The Bible says that the cherubim were created before the human family (cf. Job 38:4, 7) for a precise divine purpose which could not relate with humanity, which did not even exist yet. Moreover, Satan, who appears to be a fallen cherub (Ezek 28:14, 16), no longer fulfills this alleged scope of the living creatures. In this sense he has no reason to live any longer if this would be the exclusive aim of the cherubim existence. Then, Rev 14:3 is a strong proof that after their redemption, the 144,000 are giving glory to God *before* the

---

resemblance arrives to man that "the likeness in each instance extended only to the face." Robertson, *Revelation of John*, ad locum. When taken separately we understand that the creature-like features of the cherubim exhibit nothing about the nature of the living creatures. They illustrate the mission of the four cherubim.

7. Fairbairn, *Typology of Scripture*, 219.
8. Ibid., 233.

twenty-four elders and the four cherubim, which means that the four ones continue to live: "And they sang a new song before the throne and before the four living creatures and the elders. No one could learn the song except the 144,000 who had been redeemed from the earth."

The rest of the area to be covered by this study is that of their individual roles. Is it of any importance that the text specifies "the second living creature," "the third living creature," etc., are doing this and that? How does their symbolism affect the mission of the riders they control? In order to accomplish this task, each one of the four ζῷα has to be surveyed separately. But before this, who is the first, second, third, and fourth living creature in Rev 6:1–8? Do they have the same order as in Rev 4:6–8? How can we find out? The meaning of the cherubim's order will not be turned to.

THE ORDER OF THE FOUR LIVING CREATURES IN REVELATION 6:1–8

In Rev 4:7 the lion-cherub was designated as the "first" living creature by the word πρῶτος (first, leading, foremost, prominent). Then the second, third, and fourth correspond to the ordinals τὸ δεύτερος (the ox-cherub), τὸ τρίτος (the cherub with a human face), and τὸ τέταρτος (the vulture-cherub).

Are they in the same order in Rev 6:1–8? The Greek text testifies that "second," "third" and "fourth" are the rendering of the same three numerals earlier mentioned. For the "first" living creature that enters the picture the term ἕν[9] is used, which applies to a single person or thing, being translated "one of." Now if Rev 4:7 offers an order of the four living creatures, the first task is finding which of the four is referred to by the word ἕν? If the first one has been identified, the other three should keep the order. All the positions will thus be recognized.

First, one of the basic aspects of "εἷς (masc.), μία (fem.), ἕν (neuter)" (one) is quantitative. It designates one person or thing

---

9. The neuter form of εἷς.

The Four Living Creatures as Individuals

in contrast with many.[10] In Matt 19:5 the phrase "οἱ δύο εἰς σάρκα μίαν" is an example. Though they are two distinct individuals, the husband and his wife are to become one body. Here, one is in contrast with many. Other texts could be added as examples: Mark 10:8; 1 Cor 6:16; Rom 12:5 (οἱ πολλοὶ ἓν σῶμά ἐσμεν, we, though many, form one body); 1 Cor 12:12, 20; Eph 2:15; Gal 3:28, Rev 18:18, etc. In the range of meanings of "εἷς, μία, ἕν" it follows the idea of uniformity. In Rev 9:13, John hears "a voice" (φωνὴν μίαν) in the sense of "one and the same voice." Philippians 1:27 contains the idiom μιᾷ ψυχῇ which, although literally standing for "one spirit," means "the same spirit" in the text. Another major meaning is "someone," an unknown person or entity. This usage is found in Matt 18:24 (εἷς ὀφειλέτης literally meaning "one debtor," but is an unspecified, anonymous, debtor), Matt 19:16; Mark 10:17; Luke 24:18, etc.

The last key sense of "εἷς, μία, ἕν" is "the first." It is found in the following instances: (1) in Num 1:1 where "ἐν μιᾷ τοῦ μηνὸς τοῦ δευτέρου" (LXX) stands for "in the first day of the second month"; (2) likewise Matt 28:1; Luke 24:1; Mark 16:2; John 20:1, 19; Acts 20:7; 1 Cor 16:2 contain, with some flexibility in wording, the expression "εἰς μίαν σαββάτων" where μίαν necessarily refers to the "first" day after the Sabbath; (3) the first two kinds of texts use μία in a Hebrew manner. Now, a third feature of this word is not Semitic. But it is decisive for the question in view. There is only one instance in the New Testament other than Rev 6:1 where the cardinal adjective of feminine form (μία) appears along with δεύτερος and brings light for Rev 6:1. The text is Titus 3:10. It provides one example which demonstrates that when μία comes before δεύτερος in an enumeration it signifies "the first." The Greek in Titus 3:10 is "μετὰ μίαν καὶ δευτέραν νουθεσίαν" which means "after the first and the second warning." A similar example is pictured in Rev 9:12, which says, "Ἡ οὐαὶ ἡ μία ἀπῆλθεν· ἰδοὺ ἔρχεται ἔτι δύο οὐαὶ μετὰ ταῦτα," that is "The first woe is past; two other woes are yet to come." The language used is manifest. The word μία is not "*one* of the woes," but "*the first* of the woes." Revelation 11:14 completes

---

10. Bauer, *Lexicon of the New Testament*, "εἷς, μία, ἕν," 230.

the picture, using for the second woe the word δεύτερος: "Ἡ οὐαὶ ἡ δευτέρα ἀπῆλθεν· ἰδοὺ ἡ οὐαὶ ἡ τρίτη ἔρχεται ταχύ." The conclusion is that when μία precedes δεύτερος and τρίτος in an enumeration it definitely means "the first."

In Rev 6:1 the cardinal adjective is used twice. The first instance is in the feminine form being related with a feminine noun (σφραγῖδες—seals). The second one appears in the neuter, being connected with a neuter noun (ζῷα—living creatures). In the same text, the other usage of the same cardinal adjective appears also in an enumeration. "The first" of the seven seals is rendered as "μίαν ἐκ τῶν ἑπτὰ σφραγίδων." For the second and third seal the terms δεύτερος and τρίτος are used. It is abnormal to start the process of unsealing the scroll with simply "one of the seals" at random. That would make the further numerical indications of "the second seal," "the third seal," etc., have no sense. Thus, the conclusion is that whenever "εἷς, μία, ἕν" appears along with ordinal adjectives it also becomes an ordinal, signifying "the first" in a list.

The context of Rev 6:1–8 favors this last meaning of μία. The passage contains enumerations (of living creatures, horses, riders, and seals). When the adjective, in whatever form, appears alone it has the basic meaning of "one of" (cf. Rev 7:13; εἷς ἐκ τῶν πρεσβυτέρων is "one of the elders," although there are 24, the expression does not designate the first of them).

Usually, whenever the Apocalypse delineates an enumeration, the first element in the list is "ὁ πρῶτος" (Rev 8:7; 16:2; 21:19). However, in Rev 14:6–12 we have three angelic heralds in a succession. While the second and the third are called δεύτερος and τρίτος, the first one is called neither by the word εἷς nor by πρῶτος.[11] This proves that the first element in a successive array is not necessarily called πρῶτος, which would be more natural. Having said this, based on the literary context, "the first (ἕν) living creature" in Rev 6:1 corresponds with "the first (πρῶτος) living creature" in Rev 4:7.

Furthermore, "the phrase 'like the sound of thunder' occurs only here in connection with the summoning of the first rider. Thunder is used elsewhere in Revelation as a metaphor to

11. Here is used ἄλλος, another.

characterize an extremely loud voice: in 14:2; 19:6 (cf. *2 Apoc. Bar.* 11:3; 14:1–2). God's voice is frequently compared with the sound of thunder (2 Sam 22:14; Job 37:2–5; Psa 18:13; 29:3–9; Isa 29:6; 30:30–31; Jer 25:30; Amos 1:2), a simile perhaps derived from the theophanic imagery of the Sinai tradition."[12] The loud voice is fitted more to the lion-cherub. What follows is that the first living creature is identified with the cherub resembling a lion. Thus, it becomes possible to identify each of the other cherubim through a successive comparison. The first living creature is the lion-cherub, the second the ox-cherub, the third the cherub resembling a human face, and the last one–the fourth–matches the vulture-cherub.

THE MEANING OF THE ORDER OF THE CHERUBIM

When John describes the four ζῷα from lion to vulture, did he have a reason for this order? Does the order of lion, ox, man, and vulture have any significance? Why did Revelation change the order from that of Ezekiel (man, lion, ox, vulture)? The importance of these questions lies in the fact that if the order has a meaning, then that meaning brings light upon the mission of the four cherubim. They are in relation to one another.

Osborne sees no difference in significance even though John has another order of cherubim than does Ezekiel. For him, "the meaning is similar."[13] In Revelation, the lion represents Christ (cf. Rev 5:5) and that is why it has preeminence. The same principle functions with the list of the twelve Jewish tribes in Rev 7:4–8. Judah never had the leading position in the other lists of the twelve tribes of Israel found in the Old Testament (cf. Gen 49; Num 1:5–15; Ezek 48). The rationale for its first position in the list in Revelation is related to Christ who is the Lion from the tribe of Judah (Rev 5:5).

---

12. Aune, *Revelation 6–16*, 393.
13. Osborne, *Revelation*, 233.

Thus, the order begins with the lion and ends with the vulture. The only place in Scripture, except Ezek 1, where all of the four beings appear together in the same context and bear significance for Rev 6:1–8 is Dan 4 and 7:4. In order to answer the first two questions addressed above, the case of Nebuchadnezzar in the book of Daniel will be studied.

In Daniel, Nebuchadnezzar passes through a series of transformations symbolically represented. In Dan 7:4 he is pictured in terms of three of the four living ones. Speaking of Babylon and particularly of its king, the prophet depicted it in symbolic language as follows: "The first [beast] was like a lion, and it had the wings of an eagle. I watched until its wings were torn off and it was lifted from the ground so that it stood on two feet like a man, and the heart of a man was given to it." This experience from lion to man is a spiritual one, which is detailed in Dan 4.

The emperor of Babylon had a strong self-oriented personality, acting at times with selfishness and pride (cf., Dan 4:22, 27, 30). He was the monarch of the first of four empires that ruled the ancient world. As king of such a great empire, he became proud enough to set himself up as God. He erected an image of himself built out of gold and forced the people to bow down and worship it (Dan 3:5). This was a direct counter-reaction on the visionary dream that he had, according to which the golden head (Babylon) was to be replaced by the other metal-like empires. When the Jews Shadrach, Meshach, and Abednego refused to bow down before the idol, they were thrown into a fiery furnace (vv. 12, 20). Such was the strength of Nebuchadnezzar's ego. In Dan 4, God cut him from among the mighty ones, then gives him grace after Nebuchadnezzar humbles himself.

This experience is depicted as a transition from human to bovine and back. Because of his boast, Nebuchadnezzar is judged by God: "You will be driven away from people and will live with the wild animals; you will eat grass like cattle. Seven times will pass by for you until you acknowledge that the Most High is sovereign over the kingdoms of men and gives them to anyone he wishes" (Dan 4:32). This is the state in which he remains for a definite

The Four Living Creatures as Individuals

time: "He was driven away from people and ate grass like cattle. His body was drenched with the dew of heaven until his hair grew like the feathers of an eagle" (4:33). Nothing changed until "I, Nebuchadnezzar, raised my eyes toward heaven, and my sanity was restored. Then I praised the Most High; I honored and glorified him who lives forever. His dominion is an eternal dominion; his kingdom endures from generation to generation" (4:34); only then did he return to his earlier position among men.

The complete orbit of Nebuchadnezzar's spiritual experience consists of the following stages: (1) lion with the wings of an eagle (Dan 7:4); (2) bovine demeanor (Dan 4:32); (3) aquiline likeness (Dan 4:33); and (4) man or human heart (Dan 4:34; 7:4). In common language these represent the steps of a man from self-centeredness to God-centeredness. A human being is not really human until he recognizes God as supreme. Spiritually, persons who exalt themselves beyond God are only animals of a different kind.

The four living creatures correspond to the four stages of Nebuchadnezzar's spiritual journey. I believe that the four cherubim in Rev 6:1–8 assist humanity on its way to becoming really human. Daniel shows only Nebuchadnezzar going successfully through this process. Belshazzar and the other kings failed. However, the four living creatures try to work out this destiny for everybody.

Notwithstanding, this parallel brings a question: Why are the final two beings reversed in Revelation? Why does the array end with the vulture and not the man? Before answering these questions, we should remember that in Daniel the symbol of the vulture is not just a distinct stage of his experience. Features of the vulture are present with the lion also. Actually, the first three underline the same basic idea of denying God as sovereign.

Through their ministry the four living creatures prepare a people for Christ's coming. In 19:13–15, Revelation describes Him at His return in a language reminiscent of Rev 1:13–15, where He is identified with "the son of man" (v. 13). So the Lion from the tribe of Judah will come again as a man. He has two purposes: to reward all those who conquered with the privilege of staying with

53

Him on His throne (cf. Rev 3:21) and to depose the beast and its followers. By that time, the birds flying in midair are called "for the great supper of God" (19:17; cf. Ezek 39:17), which is compounded of the wicked.

The Old Neo-Babylonian Empire was conquered by Cyrus and his hosts. Isaiah pictured the Persian king with the symbol of a vulture (cf. Isa 46:11). God calls him "my messiah" (Isa 45:1). He entered Babylon with the purpose of taking its throne. At the Parousia, Christ comes to offer His throne to those who became man in their spiritual experience (as Nebuchadnezzar regained his position after his repentance), and to take the throne of the Babylonian eschatological empire. Christ will come as man for those who became human and as vulture for those who remained spiritually below the level of man.

Consequently, the reversion of man-vulture in Revelation does not influence the significance of the process. The four living creatures assist humanity going through the process of becoming human, a level that will harmonize with God's holiness. Those who achieve a lesser level will be conquered by Him who was supposed to save them.

We are compelled to anticipate something here about the work of the lion-cherub. He calls into action a rider, which is a symbol of Christ. All over the world he presents "the perfect man," "the real man." He gives humanity the model. Each one who will watch and follow the archetype will be human. Each one who disregards Christ will be a target for the other horsemen. By judgments these three riders, brought into action by the other three cherubim, will try to interest people for Christ—the model man.

THE LIVING CREATURES UNDERSTOOD INDIVIDUALLY

The Lion

The first living creature is undoubtedly the one like a lion.[14] "One of the first living creatures" stands for "the first living creature" in Rev 6:1, which in Rev 4:7 is the λέων , meaning the lion. The Greek expression "ἑνὸς ἐκ τῶν τεσσάρων ζῴων" (lit. one of the first living creatures) of Rev 6:1 is used again in 15:7 in a very similar form, "ἓν ἐκ τῶν τεσσάρων ζῴων." The difference is made by ἑνὸς, adjective cardinal in the genitive that appears in 15:7 as ἓν, which is in the nominative.

However, this verbal similarity does not prove that the cherub of Rev 6:1 is the same as the one in Rev 15:7. It is to be remembered that the expression "ἑνὸς ἐκ τῶν τεσσάρων ζῴων" (lit. one of the first living creatures) means "the first of the living creatures" only when it happens in an enumeration. Otherwise it simply means "one of." While in Rev 6 there is mention of the other three living creatures, in Rev 15, the text gives no mention of other cherubim. Which of the four cherubim has custody of the seven bowls, managed by the seven angels of Rev 16, is unknown. The vague details about the cherub in Rev 15:7 mirrors the general idea of judgment associated with the four living creatures.

Lions are mentioned in the Bible for their strength (Judg 14:18), boldness (2 Sam 17:10), ferocity (Psa 7:2), and stealth (Psa 10:9; Lam 3:10). It is fearless even of man (Isa 31:4; Nah 2:11), characterized by power (Job 10:16; 28:8), voracious appetite (Psa 17:12), and being majestic in movement (Prov 30:29, 30). When a lion roars it means that it seeks for prey (Psa 104:21; Isa 31:4). In prophetical references to the ideal messianic times, the lion–with the bear, wolf, and leopard–is mentioned as living in peace with the ox, calf, kid, lamb, and the child (Psa 91:13; Isa 11:6–8; 65:25).

---

14. Some authors make this identification not on linguistic grounds, but based on the detail that the voice of this living creature was "like thunder" and this would best fit with the lion's voice. See for example, Easley, *Revelation*, 106.

It seems that the idiom "like a lion" refers to the face of the living creature.[15] It is said about certain warriors of David that their "faces were like the faces of lions" (1 Chr 12:8). Thus, it is seen that the first cherub is the prominent divine warrior. He fights for the son of David.

In many contexts, the lion is associated with judgment (1 Kgs 13:24; 20:36; 2 Kgs 17:25, 26; Isa 38:13; Jer 5:6; 49:19; Lam 3:10; Dan 6:7, 16, 24; Hos 5:14; 13:8). His roaring in Rev 6:1 indicates that it seeks for prey (cf. Psa 104:21; Isa 31:4) and that "the king" is angry (cf. Prov 19:12). It is paramount to remember that in Revelation the lion is a messianic title (Rev 5:5). But when John turned to see "the Lion," a "Lamb, looking as if it had been slain" (Rev 5:6) appeared to his sight. The leonine title of Christ is deciphered by the symbol of the sacrificed Lamb. Therefore, the mission of the lion-cherub, and the rider he controls, must be perceived as a judgment that springs from Christ's crucifixion. He came to die (John 3:16) in order to save, but whosoever does not believe in the mediatory role of his death is subject to judgment. John says: "For God did not send his Son into the world to condemn the world, but to save the world through him. Whoever believes in him is not condemned, but whoever does not believe stands condemned already because he has not believed in the name of God's one and only Son" (John 3:17–18). When the Gospel enters people's life the judgment begins (cf. Matt 3:10; Luke 3:9). When human beings decide to receive Christ's death for them, or to reject it, the judgment is fulfilled. For the former the judgment ends with acquittal; for the latter it ends with censure. The first living creature calls into action the first rider with a mission concerning Christ's death. He spreads the Gospel throughout the world and starts the judgment.

---

15. Fairbairn, *Typology of Scripture*, 218. Commenting on Rev 4:7 Robertson agrees when he asserts that, "the likeness in each instance extended only to the face." Robertson, *Revelation of John*, ad locum.

THE OX

Scripture speaks of oxen as a measure of wealth (Job 42:12), beasts of burden (1 Chr 12:40), draft animals (Deut 22:10), meat (Gen 18:7), and sacrificial offerings (2 Sam 6:13). "Some oxen were raised for sacrifice or prime quality meat. Rather than running with the herd, they were fed in a small enclosure."[16] In relation to the Temple, 1 Kgs 7:25 tells us that a sea of bronze (cf. v. 23) "stood on twelve bulls, three facing north, three facing west, three facing south and three facing east."

In Rev 4:6 we find a sea of glass before the divine throne. The throne is said to have "in the center and around" it, four living creatures. This obscure expression might become clearer when we read of the twelve bulls in 1 Kgs 7 that "the sea rested on top of them, and their hindquarters were toward the center" (v. 25). Similarly, it is said that the four cherubim are in the center of the throne and around it, that is, encircling it.

The Greek for ox is μόσχος that has its Hebrew equivalent in אָבִיר. The root of the Hebrew noun means mighty and strong. It is used in an old poetic divine appellative, namely "the Mighty One of Jacob" (Gen 49:24; Isa 1:24; 49:26) in which אָבִיר (the Mighty One, the Strong One, or the Powerful One, i.e., a title of the true God, with a focus on the strength and ability of God)[17] stands in a straight relationship with אַבִּיר; (mighty one, i.e., a strong person, capable of defending or attacking, but not necessarily a soldier; Job 24:22; 34:20; bull, that is, a male bovine, with the associative meaning of strength or power (Psa 22:13; 50:13; 68:31; etc.). "It is undeniable that ābîr relates to the Akkadian abāru 'be strong.' Not so certain is the connection with the Ugaritic 'br "bull" or 'humped buffalo.' However, as in Hebrew, it may be an element in a divine name in Ugaritic. The Ugaritic form ibrd may mean "the Mighty One of Hadd."[18] YHWH is not literally "the Bull of Jacob." This would equate him with pagan deities, but it is certain that among

---

16. Youngblood, *Bible Dictionary*, s.v. "cattle."
17. Swanson, *Dictionary of Biblical Languages*, s.v. "אָבִיר."
18. Harris et al., *Theological Wordbook of the Old Testament*, s.v. "אָבִיר."

other things, the bull expresses the idea of power. Thus, one of the facets of the ox-cherub symbolism is the power of God, His mighty strength which is manifested in establishing limits both to human sin (cf. Gen 15:16; 18:20–21; Rev 18:2–6)[19] and to the manifestation and onslaught of evil principalities (cf. Job 1:12; 2:6; Rev 6:8; 8:7, 9, 12; 9:10; etc.).

The ox is the animal sacrificed at the ordination of priests (Ex 29:1, 10–14). At the same time it was the sacrificial offering for the sins of priests: "If the anointed priest sins, bringing guilt on the people, he must bring to the Lord a young bull without defect as a sin offering for the sin he has committed" (Lev 4:3). The young bull is also the sin offering on *Yom Kippur*, the Day of Atonement (Lev 16:3). In Revelation, Christians are called priests in three passages (Rev 1:5–6; 5:10; 20:6). The ox-cherub ministry has to be understood by drawing meaning from these realities.

Following the Lion which brings in the Christian gospel, the Ox brings in the sacrificial means for the Christians' investiture as God's priests and for the forgiveness of those who repent. On *Yom Kippur* the sacrifice begins with an ox (Lev 16:3, 11–14). The high-priest, as a representative of the people, makes expiation for himself. After that he will accomplish the atonement for the rest of the people. In these circumstances, if any person did not confess his or her sin in the course of the year, and did not sacrifice for it, the Day of Atonement would bring not forgiveness, but judgment. "Even in our time the Day of Atonement is considered the Day of Judgment, since it offers the final opportunity for repentance. In the ancient ceremony of the 10th day, the sanctuary was cleansed of all the sins of the preceding year, which were thus symbolically removed forever from the congregation (Lev 16), and on this day the last opportunity was given for repentance."[20] Anyone who was not right with God on that day was cut off from their people forever (Exod 30:10; Lev 16; 23:27, 29).

---

19. Here I refer to those covenantal sections that remind the Israelites that unfaithfulness is always followed by curses. See Lev 26:14–39; Deut 28:15–68; Lam 2:14–17.

20. "Day of Atonement," *Seventh-day Adventist Bible Commentary*, 2:107.

The entire period near *Yom Kippur* was wrapped in the idea of Judgment, as Webber states:

> The month of Elul, which ends with the new moon at which the Jewish new year begins, inaugurates a nearly two-month period of introspection, the goal of which is *teshuvah* (repentance). This emphasis intensifies with Rosh Hashanah, at which time God is traditionally pictured sitting in judgment, both on individuals and on the community. The days from Rosh Hashanah to Yom Kippur, and beyond to Sukkot, are referred to as the Days of Awe, for they focus attention on the majesty of the Creator-Judge of the universe sitting on the throne, contemplating us and our sins.[21]

The first living creature manages the spreading of the Gospel, which is centered on Christ's death. The second living creature handles the instruments by which those whose attitude toward the Gospel are either discharged of their faults, or charged because of their neglect of the Gospel. Whosoever did not repent at the first rider's ministry deals with the judgment of the second rider.

The calf-cherub is therefore a symbol of the continual powerful presence of God with His church, an abundant source of propitiation for God's people. The red of the horse summoned by the second living creature is the color of reconciliation, which is the ministry of Christians (2 Cor 5:19–20), and also the hue or shade of blood, the vital element of acquittal (Heb 9:22).

THE MAN

What is man? Man is a part of creation and the most eminent creature on earth. His class makes him almost commensurate to God or angels. Psalm 8:5 renders the idea as follows: "You made him a little lower than the heavenly beings and crowned him with glory and honor." The Hebrew for 'heavenly beings' is אֱלֹהִים. The Targums, the LXX, the Syriac, and the quotation of this verse in Heb 2:7 read "angels" instead of "God." However, the Greek versions of

---

21. Webber, *Services of the Christian Year*, 44.

Aquila, Symmachus, and Theodotion, as well as the Vulgate, retain the translation "God."[22] According to Craigie, this discrepancy is due not to linguistic corruptions, but attitude:

> The translation *angels* may have been prompted by modesty, for it may have seemed rather extravagant to claim that mankind was only a little less than God. Nevertheless, the translation *God* is almost certainly correct, and the words probably contain an allusion to the image of God in mankind and the God-given role of dominion to be exercised by mankind within the created order. This position is mankind's estate (the verb in v 6a implies a past accomplishment), yet the role is not static, but requires continuous human response and action: hence, "you will crown him with glory and honor" (v 6b).[23]

If we read "God" in Psa 8:5 we should not overestimate the role of man. There is still an infinity between us and God. What is clear in Psa 8 is that humans resemble God in the role they are called to perform, namely that of rulers of creation, as Psa 8:6–8 exhibits: "You made him ruler over the works of your hands; you put everything under his feet: all flocks and herds, and the beasts of the field, the birds of the air, and the fish of the sea, all that swim the paths of the seas." Brummer makes similar remarks, "The human being owes this privileged position not to himself, but to God who endows him with the capability and the competence to rule and have dominion over other living creatures."[24] This lordliness[25] of humans is very significant in the context.

22. "The Book of Psalms," *Seventh-day Adventist Bible Commentary*, 3:649.
23. Craigie, *Psalms* 1–50, 108.
24. Labuschagne, "Humanity in the Bible," 125.
25. Psalm 8 asserts that both domestic and untamed creatures are beneath mankind's mastery, and both fish and birds will be set beneath his dominion. This captainship on the part of man is illustrated in Ezek 1:10–12, where the image of the four cherubim springs from; the cherubim are described in terms of the preeminence of man. Each of the cherubim has four faces. The front face is that of a man. And as they move, they remain unturned, which ultimately means that the composite figure is guided by the face of a man. The man is the master. The only plausible reason why in the Apocalypse man loses his rulership to the lion is that Messiah is the Lion from Judah. He is now the greater

The Four Living Creatures as Individuals

The book of Daniel teaches that Nebuchadnezzar was man only when he acknowledged God's superiority and omnipotence. The four living creatures' ministry is helping people become really human. The first cherub sends the first rider as a symbol for Christ, the complete man, a man in the real sense. The second one sends the second rider who continues the work of the first. If human beings receive Christ's death they become ministers of the Gospel. If they reject the Gospel they will be judged with the sword of the second rider. The third cherub calls into action the third rider. Man should become really "man" as a result of the riders' ministry. If human beings fail, they cannot exercise their dominion over the other creatures. The fourth rider brings a judgment through living creatures or, more exactly, ὑπὸ τῶν θηρίων τῆς γῆς ("by the beasts of the earth," Rev 6:8). Moreover, the final conflict between good and evil, described in Rev 13, is between God's people and two beasts. Whoever is not man by the time of the conflict will fall to the beast taking its side in the conflagration. But each of those who will achieve the spiritual status of man will have control over the creature-enemies. In Dan 7, after the arising of the four beasts, the prophet catches a glimpse of "one like a son of man" (Dan 7:13). God gave him "authority, glory and sovereign power" and "all peoples, nations and men of every language worshiped him" (v. 14). Man prevails over the other creatures on earth.

In Rev 6:5-6 the third living creature summons a new rider with a pair of scales in his hand. It is a "metonymy for rising prices"[26] (see v. 6), thus speaking on the whole about famine, but it also reaches other necessities of the household.[27] The shortage of food recalls the curse of the fall. Genesis 3:17 says that "through painful toil you will eat of it [the ground] all the days of your life." Notwithstanding, the Scripture does not say that man, although

---

commander.

26. Schenk, "ζυγός," 104.

27. The one blown by this judgment "will have to be content with poorer fare (barley) if he is to feed his family as well as himself, but even that does not take into account the cost of clothing and housing." Wilcock, *Message of Revelation*, 71.

the cause of the famine, or any other creature, will suffer of hunger unless they did not fear God (145:15; 147:9; Matt 6:25; cf. Psa 34:10; 111:5). The hunger also revokes Israel's trip through the wilderness (Exod 16). The shortage of food was the setting for God's providence to manifest itself. It was a practical lesson to trust entirely in God.

In the context of Rev 6:1–8, the famine—literal, spiritual, or both—is a judgment. The final purpose of it is to bring back the prodigal sons of God to their Father (cf. Luke 15:11–24). The lack is the instrument of remembering the Father. By fearing the Father, the curses of the covenant will be annulled and they will have plenty of bread. The coming back to Him makes those who return really sons.

THE EAGLE

The fourth living creature is the one like a "flying eagle" (Rev 4:7). Although today there is a distinction between eagle and vulture, the Greek ἀετὸς and the Hebrew נֶשֶׁר mean both eagle and vulture.[28] The detail *"flying* eagle" leads us to extract the significance of the fourth living creature's role from places where Scripture speaks about eagles in flight.

"The eagles' hunting skill and sudden attack on their prey lend themselves to images of sure and sudden disaster in depictions of God's judgment."[29] In the OT prophets, the mighty nations of Assyria and Babylon are portrayed as eagles bringing disaster on God's people because they have broken their covenant with God (Lam 4:19; Ezek 17:3, 7; Hos 8:1). The language of the divine judgment against Moab and Edom is expressed in Jeremiah as an eagle swooping down with wings outspread (Jer 48:40; 49:22).

After Rev 4:7 the next reference to a flying eagle in the Apocalypse is Rev 8:13, where the bird announces news of imminent tragedy. Thus, an eagle in flight is associated with judgment, which

---

28. For a detailed discussion see Tristam, *Natural History of the Bible*, 173–78.

29. Ryken, et al., *Dictionary of Biblical Imagery*, 223.

fits in the context of Rev 6:1–8, where the living creatures bring in the judgments of God upon the unfaithful. The second allusion to an eagle flying is Rev 12:14, "The woman was given the two wings of a great eagle, so that she might fly to the place prepared for her in the desert, where she would be taken care of for a time, times and half a time, out of the serpent's reach." This image evokes the Old Testament idea of God's mighty actions of delivering Israel from Egypt (Exod 19:4). It also recalls Deut 32:11, "like an eagle that stirs up its nest and hovers over its young, that spreads its wings to catch them and carries them on its pinions." Here, the image of a flying eagle stands for God's mild and affable way of leading Israel through the wilderness. In a spiritual sense, God's people learned to fly by God's providence. In the same way, the eagle-cherub expresses the idea both of divine guidance and spiritual instruction for those who follow the process of becoming completely human, and the judgment of Heaven upon those who reject Christ in a spiritual sense or His followers in the concrete sense.

The eagle-cherub calls into action the fourth rider, which is Death and Hades personified (Rev 6:8). The association of vultures in flight and death echoes Matt 24:28, "Wherever there is a carcass, there the vultures will gather" (cf. Luke 17:37; Job 39:30). In Rev 6:8, the eagle-cherub announces the coming death. In Isa 46:11 Cyrus is compared to this bird, which "was the emblem and standard of Persia."[30] In conquering Israel, Cyrus was compared with an eagle. In Rev 6:8 the eagle is not friendly, but accomplishes the role of Cyrus. It happens as in the book of Daniel. Belshazzar did not follow the spiritual trajectory of Nebuchadnezzar becoming human. So he fell to Cyrus, the vulture of judgment. In like manner, in Rev 6, whoever will not attain the spiritual level of "man" will be subject to the vulture, which brings Death and Hades.

Through death, it judges God's disloyal people. Along with the other three, the eagle-cherub shelters God's covenant with His people adhered through Christ. Judgment is a fulfillment of the covenant; if the judgments never fall, the covenant is broken. The image of Israel in the wilderness is a good illustration:

30. Tristam, *Natural History of the Bible*, 174.

> In the camping and marching order of Israel in the Wilderness, there was a fixed relation of the Twelve Tribes to the Tabernacle. In the camp the Tabernacle rested in the middle. The camp of Judah, composed of three tribes, rested on the East, with its standard bearing the figure of a Lion. The camp of Ephraim, composed of three tribes, rested on the West, with its standard bearing the figure of an ox. The camp of Reuben, composed of three tribes, rested on the South, with its standard bearing the figure of a man. The camp of Dan, composed of three tribes, rested on the North, with its standard bearing the figure of an Eagle.[31]

Thus, the Tabernacle was surrounded and protected by God's hosts against any enemy. The core of the Tabernacle was the Ark of the Covenant. Defending the Sanctuary meant securing the covenant. As Wiersbe says, "God has a covenant purpose for Israel, and that purpose will be fulfilled just as He promised."[32] Sometimes keeping the covenant will involve some acts of discipline lest the covenant be broken. God remains faithful despite His people's disloyalty, even though He acts through judgment.

---

31. Larkin, *Book of Revelation*, 43. The paraphrase of the Torah, called *Targum Jonathan*, written in Aramaic, and the ancient commentary on Numbers, called *Bemidbar Rabbah*, suggests that each of the four triads of the Israelite camp in the wilderness was assigned a different banner with a figure as symbol of the leaders: Judah's animal was a lion, Reuben's a man, Ephraim's an ox, and Dan's an eagle. This tradition may have been influenced by the cherubim in Ezekiel's vision who also had four faces (Ezek 1:10; see also Rev 4:7). It should be emphasized that there is no solid biblical or historical basis for these descriptions of the standards. The Jewish tradition, however, does provide the most logical suggestion for their descriptions, particularly in the case of Judah and Ephraim (see Gen 49:9 and Deut 33:17). The reason for using this doubtful information is only illustrative.

32. Wiersbe, *Bible Exposition Commentary*, 587.

CHAPTER 4

Controlling The Four Riders

THE CONTEXT OF REV 6:1–8 depicts Christ as being worthy to take the seven-sealed book from the right hand of God. Receiving the scroll, He is appointed as the King of the Universe and receives all authority and right to rule, with His Father, the entire Universe. Exercising His full capacity as co-emperor, Jesus breaks the seals of the scroll one by one, thus leading to a series of events that takes place on the earth. It could be said that "events take place on earth because of the sovereign direction of God in heaven."[1] When analyzing these events in particular detail, there should be an awareness of the seven seals not being the events themselves; the seals only generate the events coming after the breaking of the seals.[2] Since it is the *Lamb* Who unleashes the events about to transpire[3] the breaking of the first four seals summons on the scene the four riders (Rev 6:1–8).

Before scrutinizing other aspects of the relationship between the four living creatures and the four riders in Rev 6:1–8,

---

1. Ibid.

2. It is important "to distinguish between the emphasis falling upon the new and leading fact, the forth-coming figure, and that which after the foregoing narrative is more a matter of course, viz.: the acts of opening." Lange, et al., *Revelation*, 170.

3. Garland, *Testimony of Jesus Christ*.

it becomes necessary to stress some broad considerations. First is that the apocalyptic report of the first four seals epitomizes the Old Testament covenant curses.[4] It is built on their paradigm. Second is that the seven seals cover the entire Christian era.[5] The judgments brought in by the seven seals, although sequentially introduced, are not to be seen as a relay race, but rather as amplifying the prior judgment. Accordingly, the third seal does not abort the consequences of the second one, but cumulates them. Finally, the third consideration is that the seven seals are instruments of sanctifying the church and helping her overcome (cf. Rev 3:21). The four cherubim's activity consists fundamentally of praising God and uplifting His sanctity (Rev 4:8; cf. Isa 6:2). "While they [the four cherubim] have other functions in the book (calling for judgment, watching over God's creation), all grow of this primary work,"[6] namely praise and adoration of God. Thus, it follows that their command of the four horsemen to enter the scene and bring judgments actually attests and affirms God's holiness. The riders endorse the four living creatures' profession, realizing it in the life of the church.

THE LION-CHERUB LEADS THE FIRST RIDER

A proper understanding of the opening of the first seal is crucial for determining the substance of the other three. As Jon Paulien says, "The interpretation of this seal is decisive for understanding all four horsemen."[7] The text runs as follows: "1 And I looked as the lamb opened the first of the seven seals and I heard the first of

---

4. See basically Lev 26:21–16, 27, 40–42; Deut 32:41–43.

5. Mounce, *Book of Revelation*, 151. "The present chapter, however, describes the history of the world and the church. The account is not a historical sequence of events or a prophecy that refers only to the return of Christ. It incorporates the period between Christ's ascension and return during which the gospel advances to the ends of the earth, wars devastate its populations, famine causes endless suffering, and death is the constant companion of those who dwell on the earth." Kistemaker and Hendriksen, *Book of Revelation*, 218–20.

6. Osborne, *Revelation*, 236.

7. Paulien, "Seven Seals," 227.

the four living creatures as a voice like thunder, saying: 'Come!' 2 And I looked and behold, a white horse, and the one sitting on it having a bow, and it was given to him a crown and went out conquering and in order to conquer."[8] (Rev 6:1–2). When the sacrificed Jesus removes the first of the seven seals, the first living creature, namely the lion-cherub, sets into motion[9] the first horseman riding a white horse. The fact that each of the four riders is introduced by one of the cherubim "appears fitting when these living ones signify the earthly agents of God's providence."[10] They accomplish the supreme divine salvific purpose on earth. About horses Wiersbe reflects: "Horses represent God's activity on earth, the forces He uses to accomplish His divine purposes."[11] Thus whatever they unleash through their ministry, it mirrors God's saving interventions in human history.

In the Orient, "horses are connected with war, conquest, triumph."[12] "When Roman generals celebrated their triumphs, they paraded at the head of their armies on a white horse."[13] They were not used for transportation like the ass or the camel. Therefore in the milieu of Rev 6:1–8 their role surpasses the idea of carrying the riders. They signify battle (cf. Rev 9:7, 9; 19:14, 19), but not a battle between men; it is a battle of the Lord.[14] Horses are symbolic

---

8. My translation.

9. "The translation should not imply that the horseman is told to go to heaven, but that he should come forth from wherever he is." Bratcher and Hatton, *Revelation to John*, 109.

10. Lenski, *St. John's Revelation*, 219.

11. Wiersbe, *Bible Exposition Commentary*, 587.

12. Lenski, *St. John's Revelation*, 220.

13. Doukhan, *Secrets of Revelation*, 59.

14. The text of 2 Kgs 7:6 states: "For the Lord had caused the Arameans to hear the sound of chariots and horses and a great army, so that they said to one another, 'Look, the king of Israel has hired the Hittite and Egyptian kings to attack us!'" However, God does not simulate a sound of horses. It was not an illusion. Only Satan works with illusion (cf. Exod 6:11).The Syrians perceive the ominous sound as having been caused by horses. Even a visual perception would associate God's supernatural army with horses and riders (2 Kgs 6:17). These supernatural manifestations are wrapped in language understandable to humans. Thus, God's intervention is understood as the intervention of an

of military hostilities (Prov 21:31; Jer 8:6). Wherever horses are opposed to Israel (Jer 4:13; 6:23; 8:16; Ezek 23:22–23) they mean God's horses of judgment (Hab 3:15; Zech 10:3).

Although the language is military, the intention of John goes beyond army combat.[15] The first living creature evokes a war initiated by God against His people. If Rev 5 depicts Christ's coronation as king and high priest after His Ascension, then the rider on the white horse must stand for a phenomenon that becomes perceptible or obvious after the birth of public Christianity on Pentecost. The only way to conjoin this with the idea that the seals function as Old Testament curses is to understand that the nation of Israel is judged by God through the instrumentality of the new Israel (the church).[16] After the outpouring of the Holy Spirit, the church becomes more and more an army of God against the unfaithful Israel, the first recipient of the Gospel.

The lion-cherub roaring is an expression of the king's anger (cf. Prov 19:12) and suggests that he seeks for prey (cf. Psa 104:21; Isa 31:4). In Jesus' parables, the king is infuriated by the ungrateful (Matt 18:34) and those who refuse his invitation to his son's wedding, and persecute and kill his heralds (Matt 22:7). The first living creature commands the rider on the white horse to invite everybody to the Gospel feast. This invitation begins with the Jewish people, the nation that rejected Messiah. This goes against the account of the parable. After Christ was killed, the hosts of God do not punish immediately, but are sent to bid the killers to adhere to the Christian Gospel. Revelation 5 demonstrates that the

---

army.

15. This goes against the Preterist view of the seals that takes things as they are expressed and concentrates on the literal sense of words. So Walvoord, *Revelation of Jesus Christ*, 128. Some authors even embrace both preterist and futurist interpretation of the seals. So Baines, *Revelation of Jesus Christ*, 86–87. Jon Paulien pleads for a "more symbolic approach to the seals" ("The Seven Seals," 227). First, the entire Apocalypse is ἐσήμανεν, which means "signified" (Rev 1:1). Second, the horses themselves are never understood as being literal realities. Third, the context (chapter 4–5) is very abundant in figurative elements that would make a literal interpretation of the seals improper.

16. Cf. Rom 11:14.

power of the Lion springs from his sacrifice. That is why God's first "punishment" is grace. The lion-cherub seeks for prey, that is, he commands the first rider to conquer as much as possible. The bow with which the rider is equipped has a positive nuance, too.

The Greek τόξον (bow) corresponds to the Hebrew קֶשֶׁת, which primarily appears in Gen 9:13–16 when the bow is a remembrance of God's covenant "between God and all living creatures of every kind on the earth" (v. 16). Under the bow everyone is protected from a total calamity. In Rev 6:1–2 the bow emerges also as a sign of the covenant. The main Old Testament background seems to be based on Psa 45:4–5 and Hab 3:8–13, which portray God as riding a horse and conquering His enemy and the foes of His people.

The στέφανος crown which the horseman wears announces his status as victor. However it is not a final victory. "He rode out" means that his crown does not celebrate the final triumph. The lion-cherub recalls another Lion, that of Judah, Jesus the Messiah, the One crucified. In that context, Christ is the only one depicted as conqueror (Rev 5:5; cf. Rev 3:21). The fact that He still has to fight brings to mind John 16:33 where Jesus presents Himself as the one who "has overcome the world" and urges His followers to fight the same battle. Their victory is actually Christ's final victory (cf. Rev 3:21). Ranko Stefanović expresses it this way:

> Christ is not yet an undisputed ruler of the world, however. Some people still do not accept his lordship and rulership in their lives. He "must reign until He has put all His enemies under His feet" (1 Cor 15:25). Some rebellious territories are yet to be conquered, and many captives of sin to be set free. When he "delivers up the kingdom to the God and the Father, when He has abolished all rule and all authority and power" (1 Cor 15:24), then he will wear the royal crown as the King of kings and the Lord of lords (Rev 19:12).[17]

---

17. Stefanović, *Revelation*, 228.

The victory of the Christian gospel[18] will bring the final argument of Christ's supremacy. In Rev 19, the white horse symbol appears again. Beyond any doubt, this time the rider is Christ wearing διαδήματα, or royal crowns. It is the sign of the ultimate and complete victory. From then onward Christ's mastery is undisputable.

THE OX-CHERUB LEADS THE SECOND RIDER

What John saw afterwards is delineated in Rev 6:3–4, "3 When He opened the second seal, I heard the second living creature saying: 'Come!' 4 And another horse fiery red came out and it was given to the one sitting on it to take peace away from the earth in order that they will slay one another and a large sword was given to him."[19] When Christ removes the second seal, the second living creature, the ox-cherub, activates another horseman riding a red horse. The general symbol of horseman remains; whereas the color, weapon, and mission change.

Because the number four signifies universality and completeness, the mission of the four living creatures is to be perceived as covering the entire world in a gradual manner. Likewise, the second rider's progressive mission relates finally to the whole earth, and not merely to a local sphere. This seems to be determined by the Lord's reference to the subject of the second seal, in Matt 24:6 and 7, "And you shall hear of wars and rumors of wars . . . and nation shall rise against nation, and kingdom against kingdom."[20]

---

18. "Le Premier Cavalier, s'il n'est pas precisement le Verbe personnel, comme au chapter XIX, represente du moins le cours victorieux de l'Evangile a travers le monde, par la predication des Apotres et de leurs successeurs." Allo, *Saint Jean L'Apocalypse*, 73. The reason why together with Ernest Allo, I agree and identify the first rider with the expansion of the Christian gospel is that by saying this rider is Christ it seems too reductionist for some authors. These authors cannot see Christ's mission as one of the four missions of the riders. See Bass, *Back to the Future*, 176.

19. My translation.

20. Compare with Israel's history in the days of Asa when "there was no peace to him that went out, nor to him that came in, but great vexations were

These words, coupled with the second seal, point to a general breakup of the nations.

Like in Gen 3:24, the ox-cherub is connected with a sword. After the expulsion of Adam and Eve from the Garden of Eden, God assigned a "cherubim and a flaming sword flashing back and forth to guard the way to the tree of life." Based on Psa 104:4, which says about God that "He makes winds his messengers, flames of fire his servants," the phrase לַהַט הַחֶרֶב הַמִּתְהַפֶּכֶת ("the flame of the whirling sword") of Gen 3:24 is interpreted by Ronald Hendel as standing for "a divine being in service to Yahweh, in precisely the same mythological category as the cherubim."[21] This is particularly significant in the context of Rev 6:1–8 where each of the four cherubim is associated with different kinds of weapons handled by personified riders. Thus, the tools of judgment are accompanied by the cherubim's presence, and in their control.

In Genesis the purpose of the sword was to keep humans in their sinful state from eating of the tree of life and living forever (Gen 3:22). This forced "fast" led Adam and Eve to death. In Rev 6:3–4 the ox-cherub handles another sword and the result is the same: death while in opposition to the life of the Gospel. The ox-cherub directs the sword of the second rider against everyone who

---

upon all the inhabitants of the countries, and nation was destroyed of nation, and city of city; for God did vex them with all adversity" (2 Chr 15:5, 6).

21. Hendel, "The Flame of the Whirling Sword": 672. The grammatical construction of the phrase requires an explanation however: Why is the "flame" linked with the genitival phrase "of the whirling sword"? The author continues with a satisfactory answer that "can be found in a parallel expression attached to the West Semitic god Rešep, a god of war, pestilence, and fertility, whose name, incidentally, means "flame." In three Phoenician inscriptions from the fourth century B.C.E., an altar and two hearths are dedicated to *ršp Hc*, which has been most plausibly translated as "Rešep of the Arrow." The construction of the title–divine name (*ršp*, "flame") in construct with a weapon (*Hc*, "arrow")–is precisely parallel to the title of the guardian of the divine garden—divine name (*lahaṭ*, "flame") in construct with a weapon (*ha-Hereb hammithappeket*, "the whirling sword"). As the arrow is a characteristic weapon of Rešep, so we can presume that the "whirling sword" is a characteristic weapon of the guardian deity "flame."

repels the message of the first horsemen. His agenda is to reach all of humanity.[22]

The color of the second horse is not red "in a technical sense."[23] The Greek translated "fiery red" is πυρρός, that is, "having the color of fire."[24] So one symbol conjoins two images, blood[25] and fire. If we remember that the cherubic being that acts within this seal is the one like an ox, it is fitted to both aspects. The ox is the only animal of sacrifice among the four cherubim. The sacrifice begins with blood and ends with a consuming fire. Thus, the second living creature promotes reconcilement and the judgment of the sword.

If the first rider stands for the Gospel spreading, then the second must unleash what the presence of Christ brings: "Do not suppose that I have come to bring peace to the earth," said Jesus, "I did not come to bring peace, but a sword" (Matt 10:34).[26] And here the sword is present. While the white horse brings the general propagation of the Gospel, the fiery-red one reveals the twofold aspect of it. The good news of Christ provides forgiveness through blood (Matt 26:28; cf. Heb 9:22), while, at the same time it uproots the unfruitful trees and throws them into the fire (Matt 3:10).

---

22. In Ezek 38:21, it is written: "I will *call* for a *sword* against him throughout all my mountains, says Jehovah Adonai: Every man's sword shall be against his brother." Jeremiah 25 tells of this second seal; when God has His controversy with the nations. Read from vv. 15–33, and note verse 29: "I will *call* for a *sword* upon all the inhabitants of the earth, says the Lord of hosts . . . for the Lord hath a controversy with the nations; He will give them that are wicked to the sword, says the Lord" (v. 31). Against Israel also comes the sword, "I will *bring a sword upon you* that shall avenge the quarrel of my covenant" (Lev 26:25–33); emphasis mine. The "sword" is one of God's "four sore judgments" sent upon the earth (Ezek 14:13–21).

23. Paulien, "Seven Seals," 230.

24. Thayer, *Lexicon of the New Testament*, s.v. "πυρρός."

25. Red is the color of blood that ensues from war and oppression: 2 Kgs 3:22–23; Isa 1:15–23; Rev 17:6.

26. NT data plainly show how the proclamation of the Gospel leads to divisions, especially when the Gospel is not equally received and appreciated by all members of a community, whether at the extended level of society or at the narrow level of the family.

"As in the case of the two riders following and probably in the first also, the representation is purely symbolical, without reference to any particular event of the history of the time."[27] The peace taken away in the second seal is of a spiritual nature. Jon Paulien observes that εἰρήνη (peace) appears only twice in the Apocalypse, here in 6:2 and in the introduction, 1:4, where the semantics of the word expresses spiritual peace.[28] The lack of peace is not the effect of "men [that] slay each other" (Rev 6:4), but the cause of it. Accordingly, the absence of peace is not perceived as a result of war, but war is tasted as the fruit of the withdrawal of spiritual peace.

The second seal reveals what God's providence does when the heralds of the Gospel are rejected, persecuted, or even killed. The enemies are judged and as a result they annihilate each other.[29] The Greek verb for "slay," σφάζω, is used eight times in Revelation,[30] and only twice outside of it (in 1 John 3:12). It is a verb peculiar to John that designates the quality of Christ as the sacrificed Lamb and the status of His followers as martyrs (also sacrificed

---

27. Beckwith, *Apocalypse of John*, 519.
28. Paulien, "Seven Seals," 230.
29. A very plain example could be taken from Rev 17 which reveals that God's judgment upon Babylon that is guilty of killing the saints (v. 6) consists of making the ten horns/kings of the beast, which were in coalition with the woman, supporting the prostitute and her agenda, to turn against their very protected Babylon (vv. 16–17). The "tamed beast" ate the "beauty" as a result of God's judgment. Another biblical sample is the following. The mission of the second rider is exhibited in an interesting formula: he is supposed "to make men slay each other." Apparently, this is not a regular battle. If men's opponents are those believing the Gospel, we cannot accept a military fight between two armies here. While they might be persecuted and killed, Christ's followers are not to use swords to kill anybody (Matt 26:52; John 18:11). Consequently, the expression has to mean something else. The Old Testament provides some answers. We read of Gideon's victory over the Midianites that when the Israelite army sounded the trumpets "the Lord caused the men throughout the camp to turn on each other with their swords" (Judg 7:22). An interesting prophecy of Ezekiel which was addressed to Gog, found in Ezek 38:21, uses similar language: "I will summon a sword against Gog on all my mountains, declares the Sovereign Lord. Every man's sword will be against his brother." In the future times, when enemies of Israel assail God's people, God will cause them to slay each other.
30. Rev 5:6, 9, 12; 6:4, 9; 13:3, 8; 18:24.

in a sense). It is interesting that this slaughter of the evil is under the leadership of the ox-cherub who is the animal of sacrifice on Yom Kippur. This festival brought forgiveness of sins or the death penalty for the unrepentant. Those who do not lament for their sins will be subject to judgment on that final day.

Accordingly, the main idea of the second horseman is that the preaching of the Gospel benefits results in harassment and persecution of Christians, and that God judges the rejecters. This fits perfectly with the context. In Rev 6:9, within the fifth seal, the victims professing Christ ask for vindication. They are told to rest for a little while until God's vengeance is manifested.[31] At the time of the consummation, Christ will come as the king of kings, holding a sharp sword and bringing judgment upon those having rejected the Gospel and persecuted His people (Rev 19:11–16;[32] cf. John 5:22; Acts 17:31; Rom 2:16; and 2 Cor 5:10). The judgment of the second rider on those rejecting the Gospel is only preliminary and partial. The complete response is yet to come.

THE MAN-CHERUB LEADS THE THIRD RIDER

The passage continues with Rev 6:5–6, "5 When He opened the third seal, I heard the third living creature saying: 'Come!' 6 And I looked and behold, a black horse and the one sitting on it having a scale in his hand."[33] When the sacrificed Jesus removes the third seal, the third living creature, the cherub with a human face, calls forth another horseman riding a black horse.

The color of the horse is the color of darkness in the context. Revelation 6:12 states that "The sun turned black like sackcloth."

---

31. "People who oppose vengeance on principle can appeal to both Yeshua's example and his teaching (Mt 5:42, 26:51–54; Lk 23:34). Yet the Scriptures make room for vengeance. The martyrs recognize that while vengeance is not properly within the human domain, it is a proper function of God." Stern, *Jewish New Testament Commentary*.

32. John Wesley believed that the prayer of the martyrs in Rev 6:9 is answered in Rev 19:2. See Wesley, *Revelation*.

33. My translation.

Obviously, the third horse is the opposite of the first. If the first brings the Gospel, this one obscures it. Apparently, in the New Testament darkness is associated with the absence of the Gospel.[34] Here the Gospel has been spread, so it is still present, but is blurred.

The main Old Testament background for this is Deut 28:28–29, "The Lord will afflict you with madness, blindness and confusion of mind. At midday you will grope about like a blind man in the dark." This curse is the effect of disobedience and unfaithfulness toward God's commands and decrees (Deut 28:15). It is a spiritual darkness in particular. Minds are covered by confusion and filled with lightless thinking, foreign to the Gospel, although it is the "midday" of the Gospel.

The balance (ζυγός) is a symbol used in some biblical instances of God judging or evaluating people.[35] Here not men are weighed, but food. In the Old Testament when food is weighed it means either there is plenty of food (2 Kgs 7:1, 16, 18), or extreme scarcity (Ezek 4:16). In Lamentations 4:8–9 'black' signifies hunger and lack of food. Here the black horse anticipates the picture of Rev 6:6,[36] which expresses great dearth.

The legal passages of the Old Testament covenant contain references to wheat, barley, oil, and wine. The abundant presence of these elements was regarded as a sign of blessing and one of

---

34. E.g., Matt 4:16; Luke 1:79; John 1:5; 3:19; Col 1:13; etc.

35. Job 31:6; Psa 62:10; Dan 5:27.

36. A voice from among the four living creatures was heard saying, "A quart of wheat for a day's wages and three quarts of barley for a day's wages." A quart (χοῖνιξ) stands for "a daily ration for one person." BDAG, s.v. "χοῖνιξ," 883. See also Lenski, *St. John's Revelation*, 227–28. The denarius was a Roman silver coin tantamount to the average daily wage of a worker (Matt 20:8–10). The text exhibits a condition of shortage in which a denarius, that would equal twelve to fifteen portions of food in ordinary times (Ladd, *Revelation of John*, 100), only covers the needs of one person. "We are told that a denarius would buy 16 choenixes of wheat in the time of Cicero, and 20 in the time of Trajan" (Retrieved from http://philologos.org/__eb-ta/1VisionE.htm). There will be great scarcity, therefore, when a denarius will buy only one. If the adult would have to feed a family of two members he has to change the wheat for barley which being cheaper than wheat, was rightly the appropriate menu for the poor.

the main features of Canaan. Deuteronomy 8:7–8 records: "For the Lord your God is bringing you into a good land–a land with streams and pools of water, with springs flowing in the valleys and hills; a land with wheat and barley, vines and fig trees, pomegranates, olive oil and honey." On the contrary, the scantiness of them was a mark of God's curse by which He condemns Israel's unfaithfulness towards the covenant (Deut 28:22, 39, 40). Therefore, famines may occur from secondary causes, but the first source of this famine is "the throne." From it, is commanded a deficit of bread which speaks of a spiritual deficit. The absence of bread hints to the absence of God.

The cherub with the human face, and the mission of the horseman he controls, is a reminder of the fact that man is the sovereign in creation. Nature should provide him everything needed. Man, in a proper spiritual state, has authority over nature like Jesus had.[37] The deficit of food commanded by the cherub resembling man suggests that if humanity cooperates with the cherubim in becoming human, the lack will cease.

In this dark context a flash of light remains. The same voice decreed: "do not harm either the oil or the wine!"[38] Leon Morris observes that "the roots of the olive and the wine go deeper than those of grain and barley."[39] Therefore the famine is partial. The oil and the wine should not be weighed. This would provide resources of restoration.[40] In the Bible, oil precedes recovery from illness (Mark 6:13; Jas 5:14) and from shortage (2 Kgs 4:1–7). Together

---

37. Jesus stops the furious storm while the disciples "were amazed and asked, 'What kind of man is this? Even the winds and the waves obey him!'" Jesus is a man of power. Another instance is when he cursed the fig tree: "'May you never bear fruit again!' Immediately the tree withered" (Matt 21:19). Again the disciples "were amazed" (v. 20) and when they manifested interest in how something like this could happen Jesus replied: "tell you the truth, if you have faith and do not doubt, not only can you do what was done to the fig tree, but also you can say to this mountain, 'Go, throw yourself into the sea,' and it will be done" (v. 21).

38. My translation.

39. Morris, *Book of Revelation*, 103–4.

40. As Ronald Trail comments, "though there will be scarcity, food will still be available." Trail, *Exegetical Summary of Revelation 1–11*, 154.

with wine, oil appears to be the remedy for the physical recovery of the man who fell into the hands of robbers (Luke 10:34).

The rider on the black horse has the mission to unleash a spiritual famine caused by the rejection of the Gospel that has been preached under the first rider's leadership. The famine is not fatal as in Amos 8:11–13 where people are described as seeking for the word of God, but not finding it. As Paulien observes, "the gospel has been obscured, but its benefits are still available."[41] The plague of the third seal preserves the gospel, but makes its rejecters feel the consequences of their decision and attitude.

THE VULTURE-CHERUB LEADS THE FOURTH RIDER

The fourth seal deals with another image: "8When He opened the fourth seal, I heard the voice of the third living creature saying: 'Come!' And I looked and behold a pale horse, and the one siting above it; his name is Death and Hades[42] follows after him. Authority was given to them over the fourth of the earth to kill with sword, famine, plague, and by the beasts of the earth."[43] (Rev 6:8). When Christ opens the fourth seal we see issuing forth a pale horse. The Greek for 'pale' (χλωρός) is a color "of the spectrum lying between blue and yellow, with shade more closely defined through context."[44] The word is used four times in the New Testament. One usage is in the current passage and the other three are in Mark 6:39; Rev 8:7; 9:4. In these three instances, χλωρός denotes the green of plants and conveys the freshness and life. On the contrary, the context of Rev 6:8 delineates a horse with a sickly color. Its rider is called Death, and Hades is accompanying him.

41. Paulien, "Seven Seals," 232.

42. "The personification of Death and Hades is not unusual in Jewish and early Christian literature (e.g., Hos 13:14; 1 Cor 15:55; and, in a particularly vivid description, *Testament of Abraham* 17:16–20)." Trafton, *Reading Revelation*, 71.

43. My translation.

44. BDAG, s.v. "χλωρός," 882.

Angels and Beasts

Death and Hades personified appear elsewhere in the New Testament in Rom 5:14, 17; 6:9; 1 Cor 15:26. The concept was present also among Jews, Greeks, and Latin people groups.[45] Death is personified four times in Revelation (1:18; 6:8; 20:13, 14), and each time it is linked to a personified Hades. In 1:18, τοῦ θανάτου καὶ τοῦ ᾅδου are probably objective genitives and therefore, using hendiadys, refer to a place. Therefore, since "Death" always comes before "Hades" in each of the four instances, it is likely that "Death" is considered the one who reigns over "Hades"; that is, "Death" is a "person" while "Hades" is his kingdom. "In Greek literature, the expression 'to go to the house of Hades' means 'to die,' indicating that these two notions are closely associated."[46] Even in the natural life, the grave or place of the dead comes only after death.

Death and Hades receive authority over a quarter of the earth and are authorized to kill by four instruments: sword, famine, plague, and beasts of the earth. The first three—"sword, famine and pestilence"—are frequently found together (Jer 14:12; 21:7; 24:10; 44:13; Ezek 6:11, 12; 5:12); and joined, as here, with wild beasts, as in Ezek 14:21. Three of these were offered to David in 1 Chr 21:12 when he was supposed to choose the fittest punishment for his sin of numbering Israel. Many Old Testament references indicate that these four calamities "were considered acts of divine judgment,"[47] sometimes directed towards Israel's enemies, but many times towards God's OT people. God warned Israel particularly through Moses[48] and Ezekiel[49] that her disobedience towards the covenant would bring about these penalties. They were intended to awaken the people and return Israel to God in repentance and loyalty. The reverse, her obstinate attitude and constant breaking of God's covenant, would lead to exclusion and exile. As James Resseguie reflects upon, this is not to say that God finds pleasure in the

---

45. For a list of sources about this consult Aune, *Revelation 6–16*, 399–405.
46. Ibid., 401.
47. Cooper, *Ezekiel*, 165.
48. Lev 26:21–26; Deut 28:15–68; 32:41–43.
49. Ezek 14:21.

punishment of evil, but "human wickedness is woven into God's gracious purposes."[50]

The fourth horse intensifies the work of the two previous ones. The sword (second seal) and the famine (third seal) are introduced again, this time along with pestilence and wild beasts. This recalls Luke 21:11, "There will be great earthquakes, famines and pestilences in various places, and fearful events and great signs from heaven." These facts define the Christian era in general and are not necessarily signs of the end (Matt 24:6–7) or of a particular time in history. In Revelation, both plague (θάνατος) and wild beasts (τὰ θηρία τῆς γῆς) appear later. In the sixth trumpet plague (Rev 9:18–19) and in the final stage of the great conflict, depicted in Rev 13, pestilence and beasts conquer the earth. "Wild beasts" are added as the last agency, because they consume the wounded and dying, hungry, poor, and seize those who are left defenseless (Num 21:6; Ezek 33:27; Lev 26:22; Deut 32:24; Josh 24:12; 2 Kgs 17:25; 2:24; Ezek 14:21; Jer 5:6; Isa 30:6). Only the sealed who obey the commandments of God are protected (Rev 7:1–3; cf. 12:17).

Beyond the literal sense, the text hints to a deeper sense of affliction. As Paulien says, "If the seal is to be understood in spiritual terms, it depicts by far the most serious spiritual declension yet described in the book (the climax comes in 18:2–3). It is a pestilence of soul. These plagues fall on those whose rejection of the gospel has hardened to the point of near hopelessness."[51] This is the most serious problem of humanity–the spiritual life which springs from Christ (John 4:14). If the Gospel is rejected, then Death rides towards the rejecters. The first four seals describe the consequences of sin,[52] and yet they provide hope in that reality.

The direct relationship between the vulture-cherub and the fourth rider (Death and Hades) is that vultures feed on carcasses

---

50. Resseguie, *Revelation of John*, 126.

51. Paulien, "Seven Seals," 232–33.

52. Stephen Smalley contends that "the breaking of the first four seals leads in each case to the advent of one of the four riders, who are associated with separate but related causes. These indicate the consequences of misusing power and the sorrow brought on the world when it rejects the cause of Christ." Smalley, *Revelation to John*, 145.

(Matt 24:28). So Death will hit humanity and all its captives will be "consumed" by the vulture. In the section of curses in Deut 28:26 it is recorded: "Your carcasses will be food for all the birds of the air and the beasts of the earth, and there will be no one to frighten them away." Only man can frighten those creatures and, as Abraham did, drive them away (cf. Gen 15:11). Again, whosoever is not human, which in this context means spiritually alive, is subject to the vulture.

Conclusion

THE FOUR LIVING CREATURES are four cherubim, angelic beings in close proximity to God's throne. They accomplish God's orders sometimes directly, and at other times through other angels pictured throughout the Bible as horses, riders, and chariots. The apocalyptic description of them does not provide definitions about the nature of cherubim. Although they look like lions, oxen, humans, and vultures, they only appear in those categories, and their real meaning relies on the symbol. The mission of the four riders they call into the scene of the vision draws its import from the context and relationship with the four living creatures.

The ministry of the four cherubim consists of leading men to genuine humanity, meaning that they try to bring human beings to that spiritual stage in which they recognize God as their Creator and Savior. This was the experience of Nebuchadnezzar. He crossed the way from lion to man. The activity of the four living creatures through the four riders is linked to the Christian era from the first rising of the Gospel to the last twilight of the history of salvation.

On the model of the Old Testament covenant with Israel, God brings blessing and cursing in Christian history. The former is an answer to obedience; the latter is a response to disobedience. The language of Rev 6:1–8 echoes Old Testament curses from God. He judges His people and their enemies. God's chariot-throne of cherubim is a sign of judgment. The purpose of the calamities is redemptive. Human beings in their present state cannot attend

God's presence as the four cherubim, the twenty-four elders, and the other angels of Rev 5 can. Those who can enter God's holy presence work to fit humanity for the same experience.

The relationship between the cherubim and the horsemen in Rev 6:1–8 goes as follows. The first living creature sends the Gospel throughout the earth, which features Christ, the perfect man. The lion-cherub conveying the Christ-like features of victor (cf. Rev 5:5) controls the rider "conquering and to conquer" (Rev 6:2). He commands the outreach of the Christian Gospel, already triumphal through and in Christ, but also in a process "not yet" accomplished in the life of the church. Through the mission of the church, humanity is invited to adhere to this high status. The mission of the first rider is, interpreted from the perspective of the lion's roaring which signifies anger and seeking for prey, seeking man to be saved or otherwise subjected to judgment.

The ox-cherub expresses two things in the context of the second seal. Red is the color of sacrifice and oppression. On the one hand, the work of the second living one offers the benefits of Christ's sacrifice whereby Christians become God's NT priests and can be newly forgiven. On the other hand, the ox-cherub applies the consequences of rejecting the gospel (of the first rider) against those who rejected it and persecuted those who returned to God. Sacrifice implies forgiveness and judgment.

The human-cherub also seeks to prepare men to become truly human, or Christ-like. Through starvation he attempts to bring the prodigal sons of humanity back to their Father. If they fail to return they cannot exercise the leading role of man upon the other creatures. In this case, the beasts of the fourth rider will master man, while it should be the reverse. In the context of the spreading of the Gospel, the scarcity of food necessarily means a spiritual dearth. The third cherub, however, limits the absence of the Gospel. It is still possible, through his ministry, for man to be fed and to return to God.

The fourth cherub, the one like a vulture, controls Death and Hades. Those who collapse will meet death and become the food of the vultures. Even in these conditions, Christ's sacrifice limits the

Conclusion

power of death (Rev 1:18; 6:8). Between the angelic beings there is perfect coordination and there are certain terms and ties. The result of their work, however, depends on humanity's response. For John these relations in the world above are a code to unlock relations in the world below.

Bibliography

Allen, L. C. *Ezekiel 1–19*. Word Biblical Commentary 28. Nashville: Thomas Nelson, 1994.

Allo, Ernest Bernard. *Saint Jean L'Apocalypse*, 2nd ed. Paris: Librairie Victor Lecoffre, 1921.

Arndt, William F., et al. *A Greek-English Lexicon of the New Testament and Other Early Christian Literature*. Chicago, IL: University of Chicago Press, 2000.

Aune, David E. *Revelation 1–5*. Word Biblical Commentary 52a. Dallas: Word, 1998.

———. *Revelation 6–16*. Word Biblical Commentary 52b. Dallas: Word, 1998.

Balz, Horst, and Gerhard Schneider, eds. *Exegetical Dictionary of the New Testament*. Grand Rapids, MI: Eerdmans, 2000.

Baines, T. B. *The Revelation of Jesus Christ*. Garland, TX: Galaxie Software, 2005.

Baron, David. *The Visions and Prophecies of Zechariah*. London: Morgan & Scott, 1953.

Bass, Ralph E. *Back to the Future: A Study in the Book of Revelation*. Greenville, SC: Living Hope, 2004.

Beale, Gregory. K. *The Book of Revelation*. The New International Greek Testament Commentary. Grand Rapids, MI: Eerdmans, 1999.

Beasley-Murray, George R. *Revelation*. New Bible Commentary: 21st Century Edition. Downers Grove, IL: InterVarsity, 1994.

Beckwith, Isbon T. *The Apocalypse of John: Studies in Introduction With a Critical and Exegetical Commentary*. New York, NY: Macmillan, 1919.

"The Book of Psalms." *The Seventh-day Adventist Bible Commentary*. Vol. 3. Washington, DC: Review and Herald, 1978.

Boring, M. Eugene. *Revelation*. Interpretation, A Bible Commentary for Teaching and Preaching. Louisville, KY: John Knox, 1989.

Bratcher, Robert G., and Howard Hatton. *A Handbook on the Revelation to John*. UBS Handbook Series. New York. NY: United Bible Societies, 1993.

Bruce, F. F. "Canon." In *Dictionary of Jesus and the Gospels*, edited by J. B. Green, S. McKnight, and I. H. Marshall, 93–100. Downers Grove, IL: InterVarsity, 1992.

BIBLIOGRAPHY

Carson, D.A. *Revelation.* New Bible Commentary: 21st Century Edition. Downers Grove, IL: IVP, 1994.

Charles, R. H. *The Apocrypha and Pseudepigrapha of the Old Testament in English.* Oxford: Clarendon, 1913.

―――. *A Critical and Exegetical Commentary on the Revelation of St John,* vol. 1. Edinburgh: T&T Clark, 1920.

Chevalier, Jean, and Alain Gheerbrant. *Dicționar de simboluri.* București: Editura Artemis, 1995.

Collins, Adela Yarbro. *The Combat Myth in the Book of Revelation.* Harvard Dissertations in Religion 9. Missoula, MT: Scholars, 1976.

Cooper, Lamar Eugene. *Ezekiel.* The New American Commentary 17. Nashville: Broadman & Holman, 2001.

Corsini, Eugenio. *The Apocalypse: The Perennial Revelation of Jesus Christ.* Good News Studies 5. Wilmington, DE: Michael Glazier, 1983.

Craigie, Peter C. *Psalms 1–50.* Word Biblical Commentary, vol. 19. Dallas: Word, 1998.

Davidson, Richard M. "Sanctuary Typology." In *Symposium on Revelation—Book I,* edited by Frank B. Holbrook, 99–130. Hagerstown, MD: Review and Herald, 2000.

"Day of Atonement." *The Seventh-day Adventist Bible Commentary.* Vol. 3. Washington, DC: Review and Herald, 1978.

Doukhan, Jacques B. *Secrets of Revelation.* Hagerstown, MD: Review and Herald, 2002.

Du Rand, J. A. *Johannine Perspectives: Introduction to the Johannine Writings—Part 1.* Johannesburg: Orion, 1997.

Easley, Kendell H. *Revelation.* Holman New Testament Commentary 12. Nashville: Broadman & Holman, 1998.

Ellul, Jacques. *Apocalypse.* New York, NY: Seabury, 1977.

Encyclopaedia Judaica. Jerusalem: Keter, 1996. "Cherub."

"Ezekiel." *The Seventh-day Adventist Bible Commentary.* Vol. 4. Washington, DC: Review and Herald, 1978.

Fairbairn, Patrick. *Typology of Scripture.* Grand Rapids, MI: Kregel, 1993.

Feinberg, Charles Lee. "Exegetical Studies in Zechariah." *Bibliotheca Sacra* 99 (1942) 166–79.

Fiorenza, Elisabeth Schüssler. *The Apocalypse.* Chicago, IL: Franciscan Herald, 1976.

Ford, Massyngberde J. *Revelation.* Anchor Bible Commentary Series, vol. 38. Garden City, NY: Bantam Doubleday Dell, 1975.

Garland, Anthony C. *A Testimony of Jesus Christ: A Commentary on the Book of Revelation.* Garland, TX: Galaxie Software, 2006.

Guthrie, D. *New Testament Introduction.* Downers Grove, IL: InterVarsity. 1996.

Harris, Laird R., ed. "Cherub." In *Theological Wordbook of the Old Testament,* 454–55. Chicago, IL: Moody, 1999.

Hendel, Ronald S. "The Flame of the Whirling Sword: A Note on Gen 3:24." *Journal of Biblical Literature* 104 (1995) 671–74.

BIBLIOGRAPHY

Herms, Ronald. *An Apocalypse for the Church and for the World: The Narrative Function of Universal Language in the Book of Revelation.* Beihefte zur Zeitschrift für die neutestamentliche Wissenschaft. Berlin: Walter de Gruyter, 2006.

Herodotus. *Histories.* Translated by A. D. Godley. Cambridge: Harvard University Press, 1920.

Hodges, Zane C. "The First Horseman of the Apocalypse." *Bibliotheca Sacra* 119 (1962) 324–34.

Johnson, B. W. *The People's New Testament: Selected Documents.* New York, NY: Harper & Row, 1961.

Josephus, Flavius. *Antichități Iudaice.* Vol. 1. București: Editura Hasefer, 2000.

Keener, Craig S. *Revelation. The IVP Bible Background Commentary—New Testament.* Downers Grove, IL: InterVarsity, 1993.

Keil, C. F., and F. Delitzsch. *Zechariah.* Commentary on the Old Testament, vol. 8. Peabody, MA: Hendrickson, 2002.

Kistemaker, Simon J. and William Hendriksen. *Exposition of the Book of Revelation.* New Testament Commentary 20. Grand Rapids, MI: Baker Book House, 2001.

Klein, William W., et al. *Introduction to Biblical Interpretation.* Dallas: Word, 1993.

Labuschagne, Cas J. "Creation and the Status of Humanity in the Bible." In *Interpreting the Universe as Creation*, edited by Vincent Brummer, 8:123–131. Kampen: Kok Pharos, 1996.

Ladd, George E. *A Commentary on the Revelation of John.* Grand Rapids, MI: Eerdmans, 1972.

Lange, John Peter, et al. *A Commentary on the Holy Scriptures: Revelation.* Bellingham, WA: Logos Research Systems, 2008.

Larkin, Clarence. *The Book of Revelation.* Philadelphia, PA: Rev. Clarence Larkin Estate, 2004.

Launderville, Dale. "Ezekiel's Cherub: A Promising Symbol or a Dangerous Idol?" *The Catholic Biblical Quarterly* 65 (2003) 165–83.

Lăiu, F. G. "An Exegetical Study of Daniel 7–9." M.A. Thesis, University of South Africa, 1999.

———. *Daniel & Apocalipsa.* București: Viață și Sănătate, 1996.

Lenski, R. C. *The Interpretation of St. John's Revelation.* Minneapolis, MN: Augsburg, 1961.

Leupold, H. C. *Exposition of Zechariah.* Columbus, OH: Wartburg, 1956.

Louw, J. P., and E. A. Nida. *Greek-English Lexicon of the New Testament: Based on Semantic Domains.* Vol. 1. New York, NY: United Bible Societies, 1996.

MacArthur, John, Jr. *Revelation 1–11.* The MacArthur New Testament Commentary. Chicago, IL: Moody, 1999.

Maine, Henry S. *Ancient Law.* 1861, from http://socserv.mcmaster.ca/~econ/ugcm/3ll3/maine/anclaw/chap06.

Malina, Bruce J. *On the Genre and Message of Revelation: Stat Visions and Sky Journeys.* Peabody, MA: Hendrikson, 1995.

BIBLIOGRAPHY

Metzger, Bruce M. *Breaking the Code: Understanding the Book of Revelation.* Nashville: Abingdon, 1993.

_____. *A Textual Commentary on the Greek New Testament.* Stuttgart: German Bible Society, 1994.

Meyers, Carol. "Cherubim." *The Anchor Bible Dictionary,* vol. I, edited by N. Freedman, 899–900. New York, NY: Doubleday, 1992.

Michaels, J. Ramsey. *Revelation.* The IVP New Testament Commentary Series 20. Downers Grove, IL: InterVarsity, 1997.

Mills, M. S. *Revelation: An Exegetical Study.* Dallas: 3E Ministries, 1998.

Moffat, James. *The Revelation of St. John the Divine.* The Expositor's Greek Testament, vol. 5. Grand Rapids, MI: Eerdmans, 1951.

Morris, Leon. *The Book of Revelation: An Introduction and Commentary.* The Tyndale New Testament Commentaries. 2nd ed. 1987. Reprinted. Grand Rapids, MI: Eerdmans, 2002.

Mounce, Robert H. *The Book of Revelation.* The New International Commentary on the New Testament. Grand Rapids, MI: Eerdmans, 1988.

Negev, A. *The Archaeological Encyclopedia of the Holy Land.* New York, NY: Prentice Hall, 1996.

Nichol, Francis D., Raymond F. Cottrell, and Don F. Neufeld, eds. *The Seventh-day Adventist Bible Commentary.* 7 vols. Washington, DC: Review and Herald, 1978.

Osborne, Grant R. *The Hermeneutical Spiral.* Downers Grove, IL: InterVarsity, 1991.

_____. *Revelation.* Grand Rapids, MI: Baker Academic, 2002.

Paulien, Jon. "The Seven Seals." In *Symposium on Revelation–Book I,* edited by Frank B. Holbrook, 199–244. Hagerstown, MD: Review and Herald, 2000.

_____. "Seals and Trumpets: Some Current Discussions." In *Symposium on Revelation–Book I,* edited by Frank B. Holbrook, 183–98. Hagerstown, MD: Review and Herald, 2000.

_____. "Interpreting Revelation's Symbolism." In *Symposium on Revelation–Book I,* edited by Frank B. Holbrook, 73–98. Hagerstown, MD: Review and Herald, 2000.

Resseguie, James L. *The Revelation of John: A Narrative Commentary.* Grand Rapids, MI: Baker, 2009.

Robertson, Archibald. *The Revelation of John.* Word Pictures in the New Testament. Nashville: Broadman, 1960.

Ryken, L., et al., eds. *Dictionary of Biblical Imagery.* Downers Grove, IL: InterVarsity, 2000.

Smalley, Stephen S. *The Revelation to John: A Commentary on the Greek Text of the Apocalypse.* Downers Grove, IL: InterVarsity, 2005.

Stefanović, Ranko. *Revelation of Jesus Christ.* Berrien Springs, MI: Andrews University Press, 2002.

_____. *The Background and Meaning of the Sealed Book of Revelation 5.* Berrien Springs, MI: Andrews University Press, 1996.

BIBLIOGRAPHY

Stern, David H. *Jewish New Testament Commentary: A Companion Volume to the Jewish New Testament*. Clarksville, MD: Jewish New Testament Publications, 1996.

Strand, Kenneth E. "The Eight Basic Visions." In *Symposium on Revelation-Book I*, edited by Frank B. Holbrook, 35–50. Hagerstown, MD: Review and Herald, 2000.

———. "'Victorious Introduction' Scenes." In *Symposium on Revelation-Book I*, edited by Frank B. Holbrook, 51–72. Hagerstown, MD: Review and Herald, 2000.

Swanson, James. *A Dictionary of Biblical Languages with Semantic Domains: Hebrew (Old Testament)*. Oak Harbor, WA: Logos Research Systems, 1997.

Tauşev, Averchie, and Serafim Rose. *Apocalipsa în învăţătura sfinţilor părinţi*. Bucureşti: Editura ISOS, 2000.

Tenney, Merrill. *Privire de ansamblu asupra Noului Testament*. Cluj: Europontic, 1998.

Thayer, Joseph. *Greek-English Lexicon of the New Testament*. Peabody, MA: Hendrickson, 1996.

Thomas, Robert L. *Revelation 1–7: An Exegetical Commentary*. Chicago, IL: Moody, 1992.

Trafton, Joseph L. *Reading Revelation: A Literary and Theological Commentary*. Reading the New Testament Series. Macon, GA: Smyth & Helwys, 2005.

Trail, Ronald *An Exegetical Summary of Revelation 1–11*, 2nd ed. Dallas: SIL, 2008.

Treyer, Alberto R. *The Final Crisis in Revelation 4–5*. Siloam Springs: Creation Enterprises International, 1998.

Tristam, H. B. *The Natural History of the Bible*. Piscataway, NJ: Gorgias, 2002.

Unger, Merril. *Zechariah*. Grand Rapids, MI: Zondervan, 1963.

Vine, W. E., M. F. Unger, and W. White. *Vine's Complete Expository Dictionary of Old and New Testament Words*. Vol. 2. Nashville: Thomas Nelson, 1996.

Walker, W. L. "Four." *International Standard Bible Encyclopedia*. Edited by James Orr. Albany, OR: Ages Software, 1999.

Walvoord, John F. *The Revelation of Jesus Christ*. Garland, TX: Galaxie Software, 2008.

Walvoord, J. F., and R. B. Zuck. *The Bible Knowledge Commentary: An Exposition of the Scriptures*. Vol. 1. Wheaton, IL: Victor, 1985.

Webber, R. E. *The Services of the Christian Year*. Vol. 5. The Complete Library of Christian Worship; Logos Library System. Nashville: Star Song Pub. Group, 1997.

White, Ellen G. *Hristos, Lumina Lumii*. Bucureşti: Viaţă şi Sănătate, 2002.

———. *The Great Controversy*. Boise, ID: Pacific, 2002.

———. *Manuscript Releases 9*. Silver Spring, MD: Ellen G. White Estate, 1990.

———. *Testimonies for the Church 5*. Mountain View, CA: Pacific, 1948.

———. *Lift Him Up*. Hagerstown, MD: Review and Herald, 1988.

Wiersbe, Warren W. *The Bible Exposition Commentary*. Wheaton, IL: Victor, 1997.

BIBLIOGRAPHY

Wilcock, Michael. *The Message of Revelation: I Saw Heaven Opened.* Downers Grove, IL: InterVarsity, 1986.

Youngblood, Ronald F. *Nelson's New Illustrated Bible Dictionary.* Nashville: Thomas Nelson, 1997.

www.ingramcontent.com/pod-product-compliance
Lightning Source LLC
Chambersburg PA
CBHW070513090426
42735CB00012B/2770